CLIMATE

Causes and Effects of Climate Change

OUR FRAGILE PLANET

CLIMATE

Causes and Effects of Climate Change

DANA DESONIE, PH.D.

CHELSEA HOUSE PUBLISHERS

An imprint of Infobase Publishing

Climate

Chelsea House
An imprint of Infobase Publishing
132 West 31st Street
New York NY 10001

Library of Congress Cataloging-in-Publication Data
Desonie, Dana.
  Climate : causes and effects of climate change / Dana Desonie.
    p. cm. — (Our fragile planet)
  Includes bibliographical references and index.
  ISBN-13: 978–0-8160–6214–0 (hardcover)
  ISBN-10: 0–8160–6214–5 (hardcover)
  1. Climatic changes. 2. Global warming. 3. Climatology I. Title. II. Series.

  QC981.8.C5D437 2007
  551.6—dc22

                                                                    2007027825

Text design by Annie O'Donnell
Cover design by Ben Peterson

Printed in the United States of America

Bang NMSG 10 9 8 7 6 5 4 3

This book is printed on acid-free paper.

All links and Web addresses were checked and verified to be correct at the time of publication. Because of the dynamic nature of the Web, some addresses and links may have changed since publication and may no longer be valid.

Cover photograph: © AP Images

Contents

Preface

The planet is a marvelous place: a place with blue skies, wild storms, deep lakes, and rich and diverse ecosystems. The tides ebb and flow, baby animals are born in the spring, and tropical rain forests harbor an astonishing array of life. The Earth sustains living things and provides humans with the resources to maintain a bountiful way of life: water, soil, and nutrients to grow food, and the mineral and energy resources to build and fuel modern society, among many other things.

The physical and biological sciences provide an understanding of the whys and hows of natural phenomena and processes—why the sky is blue and how metals form, for example—and insights into how the many parts are interrelated. Climate is a good example. Among the many influences on the Earth's climate are the circulation patterns of the atmosphere and the oceans, the abundance of plant life, the quantity of various gases in the atmosphere, and even the size and shapes of the continents. Clearly, to understand climate it is necessary to have a basic understanding of several scientific fields and to be aware of how these fields are interconnected.

As Earth scientists like to say, the only thing constant about our planet is change. From the ball of dust, gas, and rocks that came together 4.6 billion years ago to the lively and diverse globe that orbits the Sun today, very little about the Earth has remained the same for long. Yet, while change is fundamental, people have altered the environment unlike any other species in Earth's history. Everywhere there are reminders of our presence. A look at the sky might show a sooty cloud or a jet contrail. A look at the sea might reveal plastic refuse, oil, or only a few fish swimming where once they had been countless. The land has been deforested and strip-mined. Rivers and lakes have been polluted. Changing conditions and habitats have caused some plants and animals to expand their populations, while others have become extinct. Even the climate—which for millennia was thought to be beyond human influence—has been shifting due to alterations in the makeup of atmospheric gases brought about by human activities. The planet is changing fast and people are the primary cause.

OUR FRAGILE PLANET is a set of eight books that celebrate the wonders of the world by highlighting the scientific processes behind them. The books also look at the science underlying the tremendous influence humans are having on the environment. The set is divided into volumes based on the large domains on which humans have had an impact: *Atmosphere, Climate, Hydrosphere, Oceans, Geosphere, Biosphere,* and *Polar Regions.* The volume *Humans and the Natural Environment* describes the impact of human activity on the planet and explores ways in which we can live more sustainably.

A core belief expressed in each volume is that to mitigate the impacts humans are having on the Earth, each of us must understand the scientific processes that operate in the natural world. We must understand how human activities disrupt those processes and use that knowledge to predict ways that changes in one system will affect seemingly unrelated systems. These books express the belief that science is the solid ground from which we can reach an agreement on the behavioral changes that we must adopt—both as individuals and as a society—to solve the problems caused by the impact of humans on our fragile planet.

Acknowledgments

I would like to thank, above all, the scientists who have dedicated their lives to the study of the Earth, especially those engaged in the important work of understanding how human activities are impacting the planet. Many thanks to the staff of Facts On File and Chelsea House for their guidance and editing expertise: Frank Darmstadt, Executive Editor; Brian Belval, Senior Editor; and Leigh Ann Cobb, independent developmental editor. Dr. Tobi Zausner located the color images that illustrate our planet's incredible beauty and the harsh reality of the effects human activities are having on it. Thanks also to my agent, Jodie Rhodes, who got me involved in this project.

Family and friends were a great source of support and encouragement as I wrote these books. Special thanks to the May '97 Moms, who provided the virtual water cooler that kept me sane during long days of writing. Cathy Propper was always enthusiastic as I was writing the books, and even more so when they were completed. My mother, Irene Desonie, took great care of me as I wrote for much of June 2006. Mostly importantly, my husband, Miles Orchinik, kept things moving at home when I needed extra writing time and provided love, support, and encouragement when I needed that, too. This book is dedicated to our children, Reed and Maya, who were always loving, and usually patient. I hope these books do a small bit to help people understand how their actions impact the future for all children.

Introduction

Earth is unique in the solar system for many reasons: Not only is it the only planet with abundant water, but it is the only one whose water exists in all three states: solid, liquid, and gas. Earth is the only planet with an abundance of life (or, as far as scientists know, with *any* life).

Earth is also unique because of its climate. Mercury and Venus, both close to the Sun, are too hot. Mars and the outer planets, all far from the Sun, are too cold. Even the Moon, which is the same distance from the Sun as Earth, has an inhospitable climate because it has no atmosphere to insulate it. Earth, therefore, is sometimes called the "Goldilocks Planet" because its climate is, as the old story goes, not too hot and not too cold, but "just right." Earth's climate is so hospitable because of the greenhouse gases in the atmosphere. These gases allow sunlight through but trap some of the heat that reradiates from the planet's surface, helping to create a temperate climate that has allowed the proliferation of an enormous number and variety of living organisms.

While Earth's climate is hospitable for life, it can vary tremendously from place to place, as a comparison of the temperature and precipitation patterns in the Arctic with those of a tropical rain forest will quickly reveal. Climate also varies through time: Throughout Earth's 4.55 billion-year history, its climate has varied enormously. During much of that time, conditions were hot and moist; but sometimes the air was frigid, with ice coating the polar regions and mountains. Even in the past millennium, average temperatures have been variable. For instance, during the Medieval Warm Period (A.D. 1000 to A.D. 1300), they were relatively high, while during the Little Ice Age (A.D. 1550 to A.D. 1850) they were comparatively cold. Despite these two anomalies, average global temperatures have only varied within a range of 1.8°F (1°C) since the end of the Pleistocene Ice Ages about 10,000 years ago, when human civilization began. Throughout Earth's history, temperatures have correlated with the levels of greenhouse gases in the atmosphere. When the planet is warm, greenhouse gases are high. When the planet is cool, greenhouse gas levels are low.

That Earth's climate is naturally variable is unquestionable, and it is certainly true that temperatures have generally risen since the end of the Pleistocene. But what now alarms climatologists is that global temperatures are rising more and at a higher rate then at any time in human history. Around 1990, global temperatures began to rise at a rate unseen in the past 2,000 years, and the warmest years of the past millennium have been in the past two decades. Climatologists almost universally agree that human activities are to blame for a large portion of the temperature gains. Activities such as burning fossil fuels or forests release greenhouse gases into the atmosphere. Rising greenhouse gas levels trap more of the planet's reradiated heat and help to raise global temperatures. The escalating temperatures of the past few decades are referred to as "global warming."

When the potential for increased temperatures due to human activities was first discussed several decades ago, nearly all scientists were skeptical. While humans had undoubtedly had an impact on the planet—for example, through the creation of pollution—the thought that human civilization could affect a system as large and complex as climate was hard to accept. Sound scientific evidence gathered since that time has turned nearly all of these climate skeptics around. The vast majority of them now agree that global warming is under way and that human activities are largely to blame.

The Intergovernmental Panel on Climate Change (IPCC), established by the United Nations (UN) in 1988, is the main international body charged with evaluating the state of climate science. The more than 300 participants of the IPCC consist mostly of government and academic scientists who evaluate the peer-reviewed papers and scientific information available and issue recommendations for informed action. The first panel included many skeptics; its first report, published in 1990, stated that added greenhouse gases were likely the cause of some of the warming that had been seen but that the range of temperature increase was within what could be expected with natural climate variation. The second report, in 1995, increased the blame for rising temperatures on human activities, stating, "The balance of evidence suggests a discernible human influence on global climate." By the 2001 report, many skeptics had changed their opinion: "There is new and stronger evidence that most of the warming observed over the last 50 years is attributable to human activities." The scientists who compiled the fourth report, in 2007, called global warming "unequivocal" and say with over 90% certainty that the warming taking place since 1950 is being caused by human activities. The scientists on the fourth report overwhelmingly agree that recent changes in climate are altering physical and biological systems on every continent, and blame human-generated greenhouse gas emissions for climate change. During the past decade or so, many other scientific organizations in the United States and other nations have issued similar scientific studies.

Why is global warming a problem? Climate has been much warmer in Earth's past, and the temperatures predicted for the next few centuries are low compared with the temperatures during many earlier periods. There are several reasons that humans should not want the globe to become too warm: For one, many animals and plants will likely go extinct, starting with polar organisms but eventually including organisms in other climate zones. People depend on many of these wild plants and animals for such resources as food, building materials, and even the chemical compounds included in many pharmaceuticals. Another reason involves human systems. Modern agriculture and human settlement patterns, among many other features of human civilization, depend on very small climate variations. A drastic change in climate, even on a smaller scale than those that have taken place earlier in Earth history, could destabilize human civilization.

The effects of global warming are already being seen. Glaciers and polar ice caps are melting. Winters are shorter and, as a result, some plants and animals are changing their seasonal behaviors: Flowers are blooming earlier, and birds are migrating to higher latitude locations. Coral reefs and forests are dying around the world. In the case of forests, their demise is often due to the invasion of insects from warmer climates. The weather is becoming more extreme: Catastrophic floods, record-breaking heat waves, and intense hurricanes are now more "normal" than they were a few decades ago. Even ocean currents appear to be changing, putting established climate patterns even more at risk. According to climate model predictions, this is just the beginning.

Some of the world's political leaders are beginning to recognize the dangers of this new warmer world. In the forward to a 2005 conference report developed by Great Britain's Meteorological Office, Tony Blair, then prime minister of the United Kingdom, said, "It is now plain that the emission of greenhouse gases, associated with industrialization and economic growth from a world population that has increased six-fold in 200 years, is causing global warming at a rate that is unsustainable." While many other world leaders have gotten on board, some extremely important leaders, most notably in the United States, remain unconvinced.

Without a global consensus, the plan to reduce greenhouse gas emissions is a mishmash of promises without any real action. To reduce greenhouse gas emissions, as climatologists say is necessary, the nations of the world must come up with viable plans for increasing energy efficiency, for developing new technologies, and possibly even for removing greenhouse gases to reservoirs outside the atmosphere. The sooner these actions are taken, the less extreme future changes in human behavior will need to be. While these plans are being made, and technologies are being developed, Earth will continue to warm. Therefore, local, regional, and global entities will need to prepare for the changes to the climate system that are already inevitable.

This volume of the OUR FRAGILE PLANET series explores climate change throughout Earth history, but especially during the past few decades. Part One describes how Earth's climate system works. It also focuses on climate change: what causes it, how scientists learn about it, what patterns it has had in Earth history, and how it is happening now. Part Two looks at the effects of climate change already being seen in the atmosphere, hydrosphere, and biosphere. Predictions of what a warmer world will be like are discussed in Part Three. Finally, Part Four describes the ways people can approach the problem of climate change: from alterations that can be made to lessen its impacts, to adaptations that must be made to warming that is already inevitable.

PART ONE

CLIMATE CHANGE

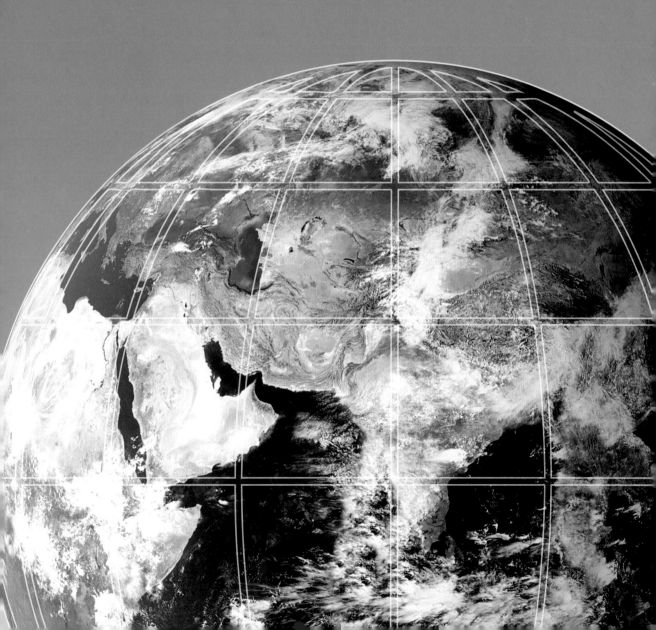

How Climate Works

This chapter describes the factors that are important in shaping global or regional climate. The Earth's climate is influenced by its distance from the Sun and the composition of the **atmosphere**, the layer of gases that surrounds the Earth. On a local level, climate is controlled by a particular region's **latitude** (the distance north or south of the equator as measured in degrees), **altitude** (the height above or below mean sea level), wind patterns, proximity to an ocean, and the makeup of its surface. The water cycle and carbon cycle are both important to understanding Earth's climate.

EARTH'S ATMOSPHERE

Earth's atmosphere is made mostly of nitrogen and oxygen. The concentration of **water vapor** (gaseous water [H_2O]) varies depending on the humidity. **Carbon dioxide (CO_2)** makes up a tiny portion of the atmosphere (only 36 of every 100,000 gas **molecules**; a molecule is the smallest unit of a compound that has all the properties of that compound), but it plays the most important role in climate change. **Methane** (CH_4) and **nitrous oxides** (NO and N_2O) each make up an even smaller percentage of the atmosphere, but they also play important roles in climate change. Ground-level **ozone** (O_3) forms by chemical reactions mostly involving car exhaust and sunlight.

Carbon dioxide, methane, nitrous oxides, and ozone are important components of the atmosphere in part because they are **greenhouse gases**, which trap heat in the atmosphere. The presence of excess greenhouse gases creates the **greenhouse effect**. Greenhouse gases influence climate the world over: A rise in greenhouse gas levels in one region alters climate on the entire planet.

Concentrations of Some Important Atmospheric Gases

GAS	SYMBOL	CONCENTRATION (%)
Nitrogen	N_2	78.08
Oxygen	O_2	20.95
Water vapor	H_2O	0 to 4
Carbon dioxide	CO_2	0.036
Methane	CH_4	0.00017
Nitrous oxides	NO, NO_2	0.00003
Ozone	O_3	0.000004
Particles (dust, soot)		0.000001
Chlorofluorocarbons (CFCs)		0.00000002

Source: Ahrens, C. Donald, Meteorology Today, Pacific Grove, Calif: Brooks/
    Cole, 2000.

Radiation

Radiation is the emission and transmission of energy through space or material. This includes sound waves passing through water, heat spreading out in a sheet of metal, or light traveling through air. Every object—for example, a human body, this book, or the Sun—has energy because it contains billions of rapidly vibrating **electrons** (tiny, negatively charged particles). The energy travels outward, or radiates, from objects as waves. These **electromagnetic waves** have electrical and magnetic properties. They carry particles that are discrete packages of energy called **photons**.

Waves are transmitted in different lengths, depending on their energy. One **wavelength** is the distance from crest to crest (or trough to trough). All types of radiation, no matter what their wavelength, travel at the speed of light. The wavelengths of energy that an object emits primarily depend on its temperature. The higher an object's temperature, the faster its electrons vibrate, and the shorter its electromagnetic wavelength.

The Sun emits radiation at all wavelengths, but nearly half (44%) is in the part of the electromagnetic spectrum

(continues)

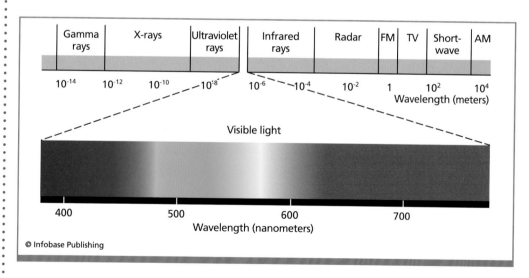

Solar radiation is composed of a wide spectrum of wavelengths. Together, these wavelengths make up the electromagnetic spectrum.

(continues)

known as visible light. These are the only wavelengths the human eye can sense. When all wavelengths of visible light are together, the light appears white. When they are separated into a spectrum, each wavelength corresponds to a different color. From the longest to the shortest wavelengths, visible light is broken into the colors red, orange, yellow, green, blue, and violet. Wavelengths shorter than violet are called **ultraviolet radiation** **(UV)** and wavelengths longer than red are called **infrared** radiation.

Due to the Sun's high temperature, about 7% of its radiation is made up of shortwave UV. Because short waves carry more energy than long waves, UV photons carry more energy than visible light photons. Earth's surface absorbs sunlight in the visible and ultraviolet light wavelengths and then reemits the energy in infrared wavelengths. Infrared energy is also known as heat.

The Sun's lower UV energy and visible light waves pass through the atmosphere unimpeded. When this radiation hits the Earth's surface, the energy is absorbed by soil, rock, concrete, water, and other ground surfaces. The energy is then reemitted into the atmosphere as infrared waves, which are also called heat. Greenhouse gases trap some of this heat in the atmosphere, causing the lower atmosphere to warm. There is a direct relationship between greenhouse gas levels and atmospheric temperature: Higher levels of greenhouse gases warm the atmosphere while lower levels of greenhouse gases cool the atmosphere.

Without the greenhouse effect, Earth's average atmospheric temperature would be bitterly cold, about 0°F (-18°C). The planet would be frozen and have little life. As on the Moon, temperatures would be extremely variable: scorching when the Sun was out, and frigid at night. But, thanks to the greenhouse effect, Earth's average temperature is a moderate 59°F (15°C), and life is varied and bountiful.

The dominant greenhouse gases are naturally present in the atmosphere, and their levels can change due to natural processes. For example, CO_2 is emitted into the atmosphere during volcanic eruptions.

However, some greenhouse gases, for example, **chlorofluorocarbons (CFCs),** are man-made and have only recently entered the atmosphere.

Not all greenhouse gases have the same heat-trapping ability. For example, one CFC-12 molecule traps as much heat as 10,600 CO_2 molecules. Methane traps 23 times as much heat as CO_2. However, despite its lower heat-trapping ability, CO_2 is so much more abundant than these other gases that it has a much greater impact on global temperature: It accounts for 80% of greenhouse gas emissions by humans.

Concentrations of **particulates**, which are sometimes called **aerosols**, vary in the atmosphere. Volcanic ash, wind-blown dust, and soot

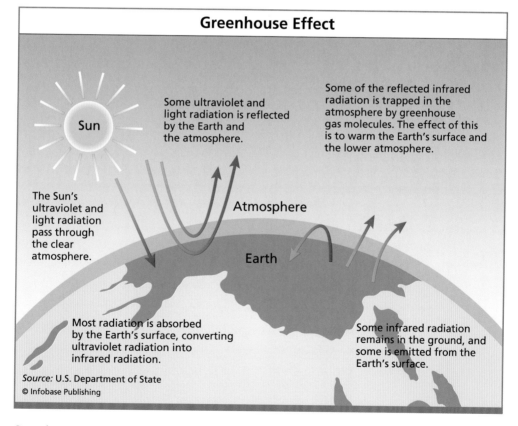

Greenhouse Effect

Some ultraviolet and light radiation is reflected by the Earth and the atmosphere.

Some of the reflected infrared radiation is trapped in the atmosphere by greenhouse gas molecules. The effect of this is to warm the Earth's surface and the lower atmosphere.

Sun

The Sun's ultraviolet and light radiation pass through the clear atmosphere.

Atmosphere

Earth

Most radiation is absorbed by the Earth's surface, converting ultraviolet radiation into infrared radiation.

Some infrared radiation remains in the ground, and some is emitted from the Earth's surface.

Source: U.S. Department of State
© Infobase Publishing

Greenhouse gases trap some of the heat that radiates off of the planet's surface, creating the greenhouse effect.

Greenhouse Gas Concentrations

GAS	CHEMICAL FORMULA	CONCENTRATION, (2005, UNLESS NOTED)	CONCENTRATION, 1750	INCREASE (%)	TIME HORIZON (100 YEARS)
Carbon dioxide	CO_2	382 parts per million (ppm; 2007)	280 ppm	36	1
Methane	CH_2	1,774 parts per billion (ppb)	700 ppb	153	23
Nitrous oxide	N_2O	319 ppb	270 ppb	18	296
Tetrafluoromethane	CF_4	74 parts per trillion (ppt)	40 ppt	85	5,700
Hexafluorethane	C_2F_6	3 ppt	0 ppt	*	11,900
Sulfur hexafluoride	SF_6	5.6 ppt	0 ppt	*	22,200
HFC (23, 134a, 152a)		57 ppt	0 ppt	*	550, 1,300, 120
CFC-11	$CFCl_3$	251 ppt	0 ppt	*	4,600
CFC-12	CF_2Cl_2	538 ppt	0 ppt	*	10,600
HCFC-141b	$C_2H_3FCl_2$	18 ppt	0 ppt	*	700
HCFC-142b	$C_2H_3F_2Cl$	15 ppt	0 ppt	*	2,400

Time horizon (100 years): The amount of warming the same mass of gas will contribute compared to CO_2 over a 100-year time span.

Concentrations: ppm is parts per million, ppb is parts per billion, and ppt is parts per trillion. For comparison, percent (%) can be thought of as parts per hundred.

Source: International Panel on Climate Change, Fourth Assessment Report, 2007

from fires or pollutants are common aerosols. Incoming sunlight is blocked by aerosols blown high into the atmosphere by large volcanic eruptions. In the lower atmosphere, wind-blown dust and pollutants reflect and scatter incoming sunlight, while other aerosols, such as smoky soot, absorb it. Aerosols have a variable effect on climate because of the way they react to sunlight: Those that reflect sunlight cool the atmosphere while those that absorb sunlight warm it.

Because gravity holds gases in Earth's atmosphere, the gases are densest near the planet's surface and become less dense at higher altitude. However, the makeup of atmospheric gases is nearly the same at all altitudes. But, despite its being similar in composition, the atmosphere is divided into layers, primarily according to how the temperature changes with altitude. The layer nearest to Earth's surface, rising from sea level to about 6 miles (11 kilometers), is called the **troposphere**. Its primary heat source is the Earth's surface, so the troposphere generally displays a decrease in temperature with altitude.

The **stratosphere** rises from the top of the troposphere to about 30 miles (45 km) up. Because this layer is heated by the Sun's UV, the stratosphere gets warmer closer to the Sun. The stratosphere contains the **ozone layer**: This is the exception to the rule that the makeup of the atmosphere is the same at all elevations. This layer, which lies between 9 and 19 miles (15 and 30 km) up, contains a relatively high concentration of ozone molecules. Ozone in the stratosphere is known as "good" ozone because it serves as a protective shield for life on Earth by absorbing the lethal high-energy UV radiation.

THE WATER CYCLE

Water moves continually between Earth's water reservoirs: the atmosphere, organisms, terrestrial water features (such as lakes and rivers), and the oceans. The movement of water between these reservoirs is known as the **water cycle**.

Much of Earth's water is stored in the oceans, which cover 71% of the planet's surface. (All seawater and a small amount of lake water is **saline**, or salty.) The Sun's rays **evaporate** liquid water from the sea surface into the atmosphere, where it exists as water vapor gas. When conditions are right, water vapor undergoes **condensation** from gas into liquid droplets to form clouds. The droplets can come together to create **precipitation** in the form of rain, sleet, hail, snow, frost, or dew.

When precipitation falls as snow, it may become frozen into a **glacier**, which is a moving body of ice that persists over time. Glaciers form when annual snowfall exceeds annual snowmelt. Each winter snow falls and is compressed into **firn**, a grainy, ice-like material. If summer temperatures stay below freezing, the firn remains to be buried by more snow the following year. The weight of many years of accumulating firn eventually squeezes the deeper firn into ice. The ice at the bottom of a glacier is older than the ice at the top. Glaciers and **ice sheets** may store water for hundreds or even thousands of years.

Today, glaciers are found only at high latitudes and at high altitudes, where the conditions are similar to the polar areas. Over 60% of the planet's fresh water is trapped in glaciers. **Alpine glaciers** are also called mountain glaciers because of where they are found. **Continental glaciers**, also called **ice caps**, cover large regions of relatively flat ground. Only two ice caps, the Arctic in the north and the Antarctic in the south, exist today. Together, they cover about 10% of the planet's surface and hold 20% of its fresh water. Much of the Arctic ice cap lies on the Arctic Ocean and is less than 10 feet (3 meters) thick, on average. Its thinness means that it melts relatively easily. By contrast, the Antarctic ice cap, located on the Antarctic continent, is 10,000 feet (3,000 m) thick and is much slower to melt. Glaciers or ice sheets can release (or *calve*) an **ice shelf**, a thick, floating platform of ice that flows onto the ocean surface. Ice shelves are only found in Greenland, Antarctica, and Canada.

All frozen water, including snow, glaciers, and ice shelves, is part of the **cryosphere**. Permanently frozen ground, or **permafrost**, is also part of the cryosphere. Permafrost is found typically at high latitudes and some high altitude regions.

When the ice melts, the water may flow into a stream and then into a lake or pond. Some of the water infiltrates the soil and rock to join a **groundwater** reservoir beneath the ground. Groundwater moves slowly through a rock layer or **aquifer** and eventually emerges into a stream, lake, or the ocean. Water is also absorbed by living organisms. Some of the water taken in by plants is returned to the atmosphere in a process known as **evapotranspiration**.

The overall amount of water present on Earth changes very little. What does change is its location. For example, when much of the planet's water was trapped in glaciers during the ice age about 10,000 years ago, the sea level was lower. But once those glaciers started to melt, sea level began to rise.

EARTH'S ENERGY BALANCE

Solar energy arrives at the top of the atmosphere as UV or visible light. It passes through the atmosphere unimpeded by greenhouse gases, but about 50% of it is absorbed, scattered, or reflected by clouds. **Scattering** occurs when light strikes particles—atmospheric gases, water droplets, or dust—and then flies out in all directions. **Reflection** occurs when light bounces from a surface. Some surfaces reflect light better than others: For example, a snowfield reflects much more light than a mud pit. The measurement of the reflectivity of a surface is called its **albedo**. Objects that appear black absorb all visible wavelengths, and those that appear white absorb none, meaning that black objects have much lower albedo than white objects.

Of the radiation that reaches Earth's surface, 3% is reflected back and 47% is absorbed by water and land. After being absorbed, some of the light energy is converted to infrared energy and reemitted into the atmosphere as heat, some of which is trapped by greenhouse gases. If the process stopped there, the planet would just get hotter, but this does not happen because eventually the heat is radiated into space.

When the amount of shortwave energy entering the Earth's system equals the amount of longwave radiation leaving, the planet's **heat budget** is in balance. When the system is not in balance, it is because the input of heat is greater than the output, and the planet gets warmer; or the output is greater than the input, making the planet cooler.

WHAT SHAPES A REGION'S CLIMATE?

Weather is the state of the atmosphere in a given place at a given time. While "hot" may describe the weather for a March day in Fairbanks, Alaska (at least relative to other March days), it does not describe the March climate of any part of Alaska. Climate is the long-term average of a region's weather. A region's latitude and position relative to the major wind belts are two important factors that determine that region's climate. The location's climate also depends on whether or not it is near an ocean, what types of ocean currents are nearby, where it is relative to mountains, and the local albedo.

Latitude

Although the heat budget of Earth as a whole is fairly well balanced, that is not true for the heat budget at different locations. The low

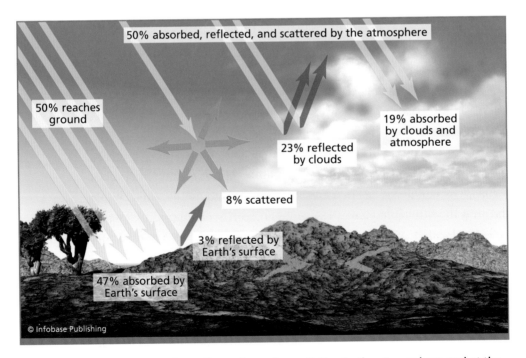

Earth's energy balance. The fate of incoming solar radiation in the atmosphere and at the Earth's surface.

latitudes near the equator take in much more solar radiation than the high latitudes near the poles because:

- ⊕ The polar regions receive no sunlight at all for months at a time in the winter, while at the equator, day length shows little seasonal variation.
- ⊕ Near the poles, even in the summer, the Sun never rises very high in the sky, so its rays are filtered through a great wedge of atmosphere before they reach the ground. Near the equator, the midday Sun is always overhead, so much more solar radiation reaches the Earth directly.
- ⊕ The polar regions are often covered with ice and snow, and their high albedo reflects back a high percentage of the solar energy that comes into the atmosphere

This imbalance of entering solar radiation between the low and high latitudes is what drives atmospheric circulation.

Atmospheric Circulation

The atmosphere flows in great **convection cells** as it moves heat from the warm equatorial region to the cold polar regions. Near the equator, warm air rises. When the rising warm air reaches the top of the troposphere, it moves toward the poles. The air cools as it flows and becomes dense enough to sink at latitudes of about 30°N or 30°S. When this air reaches the surface, it is sucked toward the equator by the rising air, warming as it goes. The horizontal motion of air along the ground creates wind. When the air returns to the equator, the convection cell is complete. Convection cells are located at latitudes between 30°N and 30°S, 50° to 60°N, and 50° to 60°S, and at the poles. Earth's rotation influences the direction air moves by means of the **Coriolis effect**, which is the tendency of a freely moving object to appear to move to the right in the northern hemisphere and to the left in the southern hemisphere due to Earth's rotation.

Atmospheric circulation cells set the framework for a region's climate. Where the air is rising or sinking—at the equator, at 30°, at 50° to 60°, and at the poles—there is little wind. Because air cools as

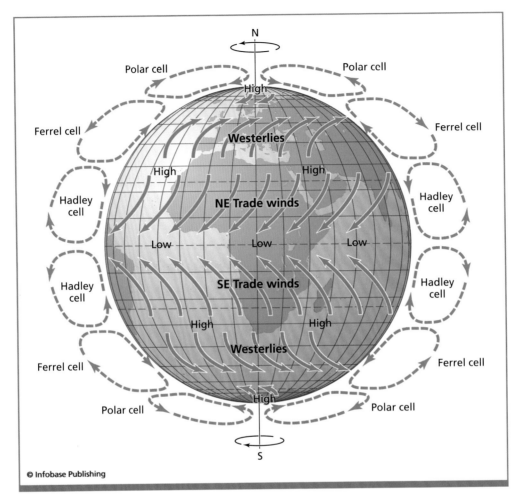

The six-cell model of global air circulation, showing the locations of high and low pressure cells and the directions of the major wind belts on the Earth's surface.

it rises, and cool air can hold less moisture than warm air, locations where air rises (low pressure zones near the equator and at 50° to 60°) have high levels of precipitation. Locations where the air sinks (high pressure zones near 30°) experience more evaporation than precipitation. Air moves horizontally from high to low pressure zones, forming the major wind belts, which include the trade winds, between the equator and 30°N and 30°S; the westerlies, between 30°N and 30°S and 50° to 60°N and 50° to 60°S; and the polar winds. Convection cells are the framework for atmospheric circulation, although other factors also influence the force and direction of wind.

The Effects of the Ocean on Climate

Ocean currents transport heat around the Earth and influence regional climate as they warm or cool the air above the seas. The major surface ocean currents travel in the same direction as the major wind belts because the wind pushes the seawater. For example, the westerly winds drag North Pacific water from west to east, while the trade winds move surface currents from east to west both north and south of the equator. When these currents run into continents, the Coriolis effect causes them to turn right in the Northern Hemisphere and left in the Southern Hemisphere. The currents flow along the continents until they run into an east-west moving current going in the opposite direction. The result is surface currents that travel in loops called **gyres**, which rotate clockwise in the Northern Hemisphere and counterclockwise in the Southern Hemisphere.

The North Atlantic gyre has an enormous influence on the climate of northern Europe. At the southern part of this gyre, seawater is warmed by the Sun as it moves from east to west across the equator. When it hits the Americas, the current turns right (north) and becomes the Gulf Stream, a swift warm water current that raises air temperatures along the eastern United States and southeastern Canada. At the northern part of the gyre, the Gulf Stream swings right, away from North America and toward Europe, where it divides into two segments. One segment moves south toward Africa, completing the gyre, while the other moves north, along Great Britain and Norway. The northern current, called the North Atlantic Drift, brings fairly warm Gulf Stream water into the northern latitudes. This current creates air temperatures in the North Atlantic that are 5°F to 11°F (3° to 6°C) warmer than those of other regions at the same latitudes. As a result, although London is at 51° north latitude, several degrees farther north than Quebec, Canada, its climate is much more temperate: Rain instead of snow predominates in London during winter. Besides influencing air temperature, ocean currents also affect precipitation levels because warm water currents bring more moisture and therefore more rain to a region than do cold currents.

Ocean currents also distribute heat from surface waters into the deep ocean. North Atlantic water sinks into the deep sea because sea ice formation removes the fresh water and leaves behind water that is very saline and very cold. (Water density is a function of temperature and salinity; cold saline water is densest.) After sinking, the water flows toward Antarctica and circulates through the deep sea until it rises to the surface at various locations, mostly near continents. The vertical movement of ocean currents is known as **thermohaline circulation** (*thermo* means heat and *haline* means salt), which is very sensitive to surface ocean temperatures and surface ocean salinity. Thermohaline circulation drives **Atlantic meridional overturning**, which brings warm surface waters (such as the Gulf Stream) north and pushes cold deep waters south. A region's location relative to surface ocean currents strongly influences its climate.

Simply being near an ocean also influences an area's climate. A surface that is covered by earth materials (rock, sand, and soil) will become hotter than one that is covered with water, even if the two surfaces are exposed to the same amount of solar radiation. This is because earth materials have higher **specific heat**, which is the amount of energy needed to raise the temperature of one gram of material by 1.8°F (1°C). Because land absorbs and releases heat more readily than water, the air temperature over land is much more variable: Summer temperatures and daytime temperatures are hotter, and winter and nighttime temperatures are colder. A climate in a region with no nearby ocean is considered a continental climate and will therefore experience a great deal of temperature variation. A climate with a nearby ocean that moderates its temperatures, both daily and seasonally, is a considered a maritime climate. Maritime climates are even more moderate if the prevailing winds come off the sea. The mild summers and winters of San Francisco, California, when compared to the extreme seasons of Wichita, Kansas (both cities are at latitude 37°N), are testament to the moderating effects of the Pacific Ocean.

Land can only store heat near the surface, but the oceans can store heat at great depth. This is why land temperatures appear to rise more than ocean temperatures. Water has high **heat capacity**, which means that it can absorb large amounts of heat with very little temperature change.

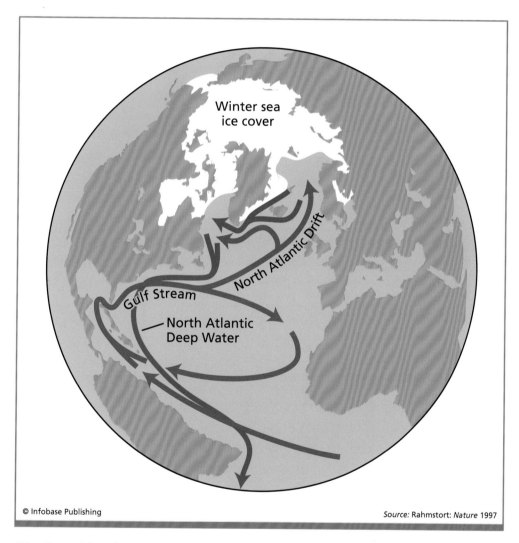

Source: Rahmstort: *Nature* 1997

Atlantic meridional overturning. Warm water from the equatorial region flows up eastern North America as the Gulf Stream. The current splits, with a portion returning to the equator, and another portion flowing northward as the North Atlantic Drift and bringing warmth to Great Britain and northern Europe. In the North Atlantic, sea ice formation and low temperatures make the surface waters cold and dense so that they sink, becoming North Atlantic deep water.

Altitude and Albedo

Altitude affects the climate of a region as air temperature decreases with height above sea level. For example, the high reaches of Mt. Kilimanjaro, Tanzania, at the equator, support glaciers even though the surrounding countryside down below is swelteringly hot.

Common Surfaces and Their Albedo

SURFACE	ALBEDO (%)
Earth average	30
Moon average	7
Fresh snow	90
Antarctica	80
Clouds	0 to high 70s (jet contrails)
Desert	25
Beach	25
Grassy field	20
Farmland	15
Deciduous forest	13
City, tropical region	12
Swampland	9 to 14
Pine forest in winter, 45°N*	9
City, northern region	7
Bare dirt	5 to 40, depending on color
Ocean	3.5

*Lowest albedo in a natural land environment due to color of trees and scattering of sunlight by trees.

Source: C. Donald Ahrens, Meteorology Today: An Introduction to Weather, Climate, and the Environment, *Brooks/Cole, 2000.*

Albedo affects climate locally and globally. A location with high albedo, such as a glacier, reflects most of its incoming solar radiation and so remains cool. If the ice melts, the swamp that replaces it will have much lower albedo, and the ground will absorb heat. In that latter scenario, the warm swamp warms the air above it, which may alter atmospheric circulation and affect global climate.

THE CARBON CYCLE

Understanding carbon is extremely important to understanding climate. The two most important greenhouse gases, carbon dioxide and methane, are carbon based. Carbon only affects climate when it is in the atmosphere, but to understand the effect of carbon-based gases on climate, it is necessary to understand how these gases move through all of Earth's major reservoirs: the atmosphere, biosphere (living things), geosphere (the solid Earth), and hydrosphere (fresh water and oceans). The **carbon cycle** describes the movement of carbon between these different reservoirs.

Carbon dioxide continually moves in and out of the atmosphere. CO_2 leaves the atmosphere primarily through **photosynthesis**, the process in which plants take CO_2 and water (H_2O) to produce sugar ($C_6H_{12}O_6$) and oxygen (O_2). The simplified chemical reaction for photosynthesis is:

$$6CO_2 + 12H_2O + \text{solar energy} = C_6H_{12}O_6 + 6O_2 + 6H_2O$$

The amount of food energy created by photosynthesis is known as **primary productivity**. Photosynthesis is performed primarily by land plants and tiny marine plants called **phytoplankton** in the upper layer of the ocean. These organisms are called **producers**. Photosynthesizers use CO_2 from the atmosphere to build their body tissue. (**Zooplankton** are tiny marine animals that eat phytoplankton. **Plankton** refers to both phytoplankton and zooplankton.)

Carbon may be stored in a single reservoir so that it is, at least temporarily, no longer part of the carbon cycle. This is called **carbon sequestration**. Some important reservoirs for carbon sequestration

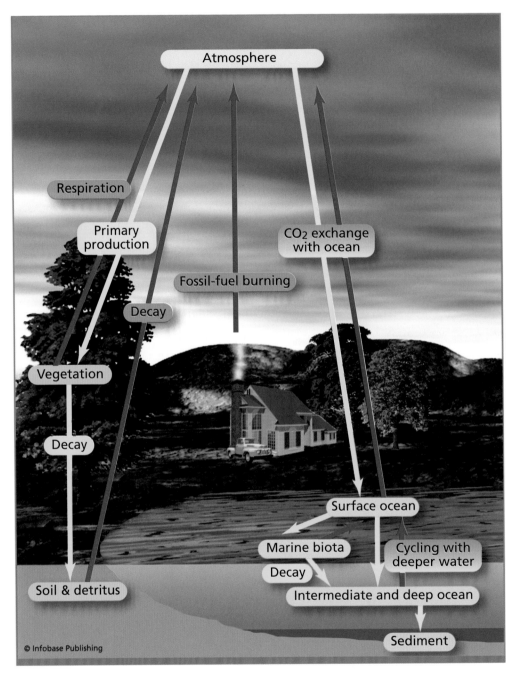

The carbon cycle, showing inputs of carbon into the atmosphere and outputs of carbon from the atmosphere.

are swamps and forests. Ancient plants and plankton are converted by earth processes into **fossil fuels**—oil, gas, coal, and others—which also sequester large quantities of carbon. (Currently, about 85% of primary power generation comes from fossil fuels.)

Carbon also freely enters the ocean. CO_2 readily dissolves in seawater, making the oceans into enormous carbon reservoirs. Marine organisms use CO_2 from seawater to make **carbonate** shells and other hard parts. (A carbonate compound contains the carbonate **ion** CO_3. Most carbonates, including calcite and limestone, are calcium carbonates [$CaCO_3$].) After the organisms die, some of the shells sink into the deep ocean, where they are buried by **sediments**. (Sediments are fragments of rocks, shells, and living organisms that range in size from dust to boulders.) This carbonate may later become part of a rock, often limestone. The balance between the acidity of seawater and the dissolution of carbonates keeps the pH of ocean water in balance. (An **acid** has free hydrogen ions and can be neutralized by an alkaline substance. The measure of the balance between a solution's acidity and its alkalinity is called its **pH**.) Earth processes transport some of these sediments deeper into the planet's interior.

The carbon cycle also brings carbon back into the atmosphere. Carbon dioxide reenters the atmosphere when the processes described above are reversed, as by **respiration**, fire, decomposition, or volcanic eruptions. In respiration, animals and plants use oxygen to convert sugar created in photosynthesis into energy that they can use. The chemical equation for respiration looks like photosynthesis in reverse:

$$C_6H_{12}O_6 + 6O_2 = 6CO_2 + 6H_2O + \text{useable energy}$$

Note that in photosynthesis, CO_2 is converted to O_2, while in respiration, O_2 is converted to CO_2.

CO_2 sequestered in sediments, rock, Earth's interior, or living things can be rereleased into the atmosphere. For example, if carbonate rock is exposed to the atmosphere, the rock weathers and releases its CO_2 into the atmosphere. Volcanic eruptions tap CO_2 sequestered in Earth's interior and inject it into the atmosphere. Forests lose carbon to the atmosphere if they decompose or are burned. CO_2 is rereleased into the atmosphere when fossil fuels are burned. Scientists estimate that recoverable fossil fuel reserves contain about five times as much carbon as is currently in the atmosphere.

Water temperature affects the ability of the oceans to store carbon. Cold water holds more gas, so cold seawater absorbs CO_2 from the atmosphere. Conversely, gases bubble up as seawater warms and re-enter the atmosphere.

Like carbon dioxide, methane enters the atmosphere in a variety of ways. Methane forms primarily as single-celled **bacteria** and other organisms break down organic substances—sewage, plant material, or food—in the absence of oxygen. Methane enters the atmosphere during volcanic eruptions and from mud volcanoes.

Methane is the primary component of **natural gas**, which forms in a process that is similar to the process that forms other fossil fuels. Natural gas formation removes methane from the atmosphere. The methane is rereleased into the atmosphere when natural gas is burned. The atmosphere also loses methane when CH_4 undergoes a reaction with hydroxyl (OH) ions. Over time, atmospheric methane breaks down to form CO_2. Living plants may also add methane to the atmosphere, although scientists are just beginning to explore this idea.

Methane is found in offshore sediments in enormous quantities as **methane hydrates**. These compounds develop at depths of 660 to 1,650 feet (200 to 500 m) below sea level when decomposed organic matter contacts cold water at the high pressures found deep in layered sediments. Water molecules form an icy cage (a hydrate) that contains a methane molecule. The molecule's structure is unstable; when the pressure is removed from the hydrate, the structure collapses, and the methane escapes. Methane hydrates can also be used as fuel, although the technology for mining them and harnessing their energy has not yet been developed. Thousands of gigatons of methane, equal to the world's total amount of coal, are located in the oceans.

WRAP-UP

Earth's climate is a complex system. In any location, climate is determined by latitude, proximity to an ocean, position relative to atmospheric and oceanic currents, altitude and albedo, plus other factors. One of the most important determinants of Earth's global climate is atmospheric greenhouse gases. Because greenhouse gases trap some of the heat that radiates from Earth's surface, an increase in their abundance causes **global warming**, the ongoing rise in average global temperatures. Due to their abundance, the carbon-based gases carbon dioxide and methane are the most important greenhouse gases. Carbon cycles in and out of the atmosphere: It is sequestered in various reservoirs, such as fossil fuels and trees, but it is also released back into the atmosphere when, for example, those commodities are burned. Small changes in any of the features that regulate climate may cause the climate to change locally or globally. These changes and their effects will be described in the next two chapters.

Natural Causes
of Climate Change

Throughout Earth history, the climate has changed globally and locally and throughout nearly all time periods. Climate change has many natural causes, such as variations in the amount of solar radiation that come in to Earth's system, the position of Earth relative to Sun, the position of continents relative to the equator, and even whether the continents are together or apart. Smaller factors that are important over shorter time periods are volcanic eruptions and asteroid impacts. This chapter also discusses how natural climate oscillations caused by interactions of the atmosphere and oceans take place on time scales of decades or years.

SOLAR VARIATION

Solar radiation is so important to Earth's climate that changes in sunlight could bring about changes in climate. These changes could occur over long or short time frames.

Since the Sun was born, 4.55 billion years ago, the star has been very gradually increasing its amount of radiation so that it is now 20%

to 30% more intense than it once was. Even so, Earth was about the same temperature back then as it is today because CO_2 levels were much higher. The resultant greenhouse warming made up for the smaller amount of solar radiation. The average solar radiation reaching Earth has changed only slightly during the past few hundred million years.

Sunspots—magnetic storms that appear as dark, relatively cool regions on the Sun's surface—represent short-term variations in solar radiation. Sunspot activity varies on an 11-year cycle. When the number of sunspots is high, solar radiation is also relatively high. Satellite data collected over the past two sunspot cycles has shown a variation in solar radiation of only up to 0.1%, probably too little to affect Earth's climate. However, during the time between 1645 and 1715, known as the Maunder Minimum, there were few sunspots. This period correlates with a portion of the **Little Ice Age (LIA)**, but is not necessarily the cause.

The amount of solar radiation that reaches Earth's atmosphere is known as **insolation**. The rate of insolation is affected by the amount of clouds, dust, ash, and **air pollution** in the atmosphere. Rapid changes in insolation can also be caused by volcanic eruptions and asteroid impacts.

MILANKOVITCH CYCLES

Significant variations in the amount of solar radiation striking the planet can be the result of differences in Earth's position relative to the Sun. Solar radiation in a particular location can vary as much as 25%, although the global average varies much less. Nonetheless, large deviations in solar radiation have profoundly influenced global climate through Earth history by, for example, initiating ice ages. The patterns of variation are described by the **Milankovitch theory**, named for the Serbian geophysicist Milutin Milankovitch, who proposed the idea in the 1930s.

The Milankovitch theory describes three variations in Earth's position relative to the Sun:

⊕ Earth's orbit around the Sun changes from a more circular route to a more elliptical one on a cycle of about 90,000 to

100,000 years: This variation is called *eccentricity*. When the orbit is more circular, as it is now, the amount of solar radiation the Earth receives during a year differs by only 6%. When the orbit is at its most elliptical, solar radiation varies by between 20% and 30%. Such a large variation in solar radiation profoundly affects global climate.

⊕ Earth also wobbles on its axis of rotation. This wobble is known as *precession*. Currently, Earth's axis of rotation points toward Polaris, the North Star. Precession moves the orientation of the axis of rotation so that in about 12,000 years it will point toward the star Vega, which will then be the new north star. At that time, the Northern Hemisphere's summer will take place when Earth is closest to the Sun (unlike now) and Northern Hemisphere winter will be when Earth is farthest from the Sun (also unlike now). As a result, winters will be much colder and summers will be much warmer than they are today. However, precession will continue, and in 27,000 years Polaris will again be the North Star.

⊕ Earth's seasons are caused by the 23.5° angle of the planet's axis of rotation. As Earth orbits the Sun, the tilt of the planet's axis relative to the Sun changes throughout the year. The Northern Hemisphere is tilted the most toward the Sun on summer solstice (June 21 or 22), when the Sun's rays reach the farthest north. The Northern Hemisphere is tilted farthest away from the Sun on winter solstice (December 21 or 22). But this axial tilt (or *obliquity*) is not constant. Over a period of about 41,000 years it varies between 22.1 and 24.5 degrees. The smaller the planet's tilt, the less variation there is between summer and winter in the middle and high latitudes. When winters are milder and summers are cooler in the high latitudes, glaciers are more likely to form.

The superimposition of these three variations results in a variation in climate pattern of about 100,000 years. Scientists have shown that the climate in the past several hundred thousand years, and particularly the

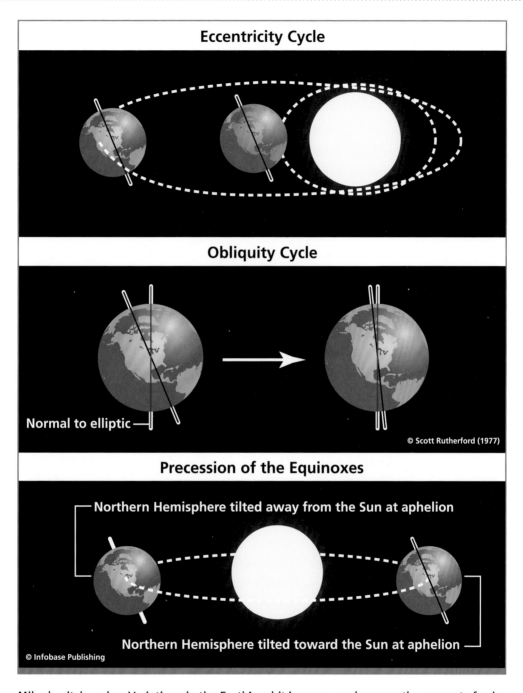

Milankovitch cycles. Variations in the Earth's orbit increase or decrease the amount of solar radiation the planet receives. The three variations are (1) eccentricity: how elliptical the planet's orbit is; (2) obliquity: the angle of the Earth's axis of rotation; and (3) precession: the amount the Earth wobbles on its axis of rotation.

glacial advances of the **Pleistocene Ice Ages,** has been closely associated with the 100,000-year pattern of these Milankovitch cycles.

PLATE TECTONICS

The movements of the continents and the processes that cause them are described by the theory of **plate tectonics.** Because plate movements determine the shapes and sizes of continents and ocean basins, plate tectonics can have a long-term effect on climate. When all the continents are joined into one supercontinent, as they were 225 million years ago (MYA), most of the land area is far from the oceans, and a harsher continental climate dominates. But when the continents are separate, as they are today, ocean currents are better able to distribute heat because more of the land surface is near an ocean. This results in less extreme global and regional climate. Plate motions also reinforce Milankovitch cycles. If continents are located near the poles, and the amount of solar radiation reaching the poles is low, snow and ice will accumulate, which is favorable to planetary cooling and perhaps the initiation of an ice age.

Plate tectonics cause geologic activity that, in turn, influences climate. When limestone or other carbonate rocks push up to form mountain ranges, or when tectonic activity lowers sea level so that more carbonate rocks are exposed, these rocks undergo a weathering process that releases the greenhouse gas CO_2 into the atmosphere. But if plate tectonics processes cause the sea level to rise, carbonate breakdown decreases.

Plate tectonic movements cause most volcanic eruptions. These can have short- or long-term effects on the climate. The aerosols released by the 1991 eruption of Mt. Pinatubo in the Philippines reduced global insolation by 5% and decreased average global temperature by about 0.9°F (0.5°C) the following year. As a result, the United States had its third wettest and coldest summer in 77 years.

In addition, extremely rare, but incredibly large, eruptions of **flood basalts** produce very fluid lava that covers millions of square miles (km) with extremely thick flows. These violent eruptions propel ash,

Mass Extinctions

During a mass extinction, 25% or more of all of Earth's species go extinct during a geologically brief period. Mass extinctions have mostly been caused by asteroid impacts, massive volcanic eruptions, or climate change. Since life began to flourish 600 million years ago, there here have been at least five major mass extinction events and many smaller ones.

Many scientists agree that the mass extinction that occurred at the end of the Cretaceous Period 65 MYA was brought on by a strike from an asteroid 6 miles (10 km) wide. By the end of this period, two-thirds of Earth's species, including the dinosaurs, were gone. The story scientists have pieced together is frightening. The asteroid struck water, causing giant tsunamis that flooded coastal regions, even thousands of miles away. Dust and gas flew skyward and then coalesced into balls that fell back to earth as fireballs. This released so much energy that the atmosphere was as hot as a kitchen oven on broil. Animals roasted and forests burned. Shortly afterward, dust and smoke blocked out sunlight and the planet froze. The darkness triggered a major decline in photosynthesis, causing the plants and animals that survived the initial impact to starve. Gases that were released into the atmosphere from the limestone rock that the asteroid hit formed acid rain, which dis-

solved phytoplankton shells and caused the oceans' **food webs** to collapse. (A food web is the complex set of food interactions between organisms in an **ecosystem**. An ecosystem is composed of the plants and animals of a region and the resources they need to live.) Carbon from the limestone mixed with oxygen in the atmosphere to form CO_2, which brought about years of intense greenhouse warming. Scientists think that other mass extinction events may also have been caused by asteroid impacts, including the extinction that took place 250 million years ago, at the end of the Permian Period, during which 95% of Earth's species perished.

Floods basalts can also trigger mass extinctions by causing global cooling, global warming, or acid rain. Two of the largest flood basalts, the Deccan Traps of India and the Siberian Traps, (which occurred 65 million and 250 million years ago, respectively) date to the times of the two massive extinctions mentioned above. Scientists hypothesize that the eruptions first caused the climate to cool, due to the particulates blocking the Sun, and then to warm, due to high atmospheric concentrations of volcanic gases, such as sulfur, which brought about global warming. Whether each extinction event was caused by one phenomenon—a flood

(continues)

(continues)
basalt eruption or an asteroid impact—or by a combination of the two is a matter of much debate among scientists.

Even without asteroid impacts and volcanic eruptions, climate change can cause mass extinctions. Planetary cool- ing resulting in an immense glaciation is thought to have caused the extinction of nearly 80% of the planet's species 544 million years ago. Climate change is at least partially responsible for the extinc- tions of large animals that came at the end of the ice ages 10,000 years ago.

dust, and aerosols into the stratosphere, block sunlight, and cause global cooling. Conversely, the eruptions release CO_2, which causes greenhouse warming. If the basalt eruption is rich in sulfur gases, the sulfur combines with water vapor to produce sulfuric acid haze. Sulfur- and nitrogen-oxide gases in the atmosphere combine with water vapor to form sulfuric and nitric acids, which later fall as **acid rain**, rain that is more acidic than natural rainwater. Acid rain can damage plants and dissolve shells and have many other negative effects.

Similarly, asteroid impacts can cause climate change as enormous amounts of particles are thrust into the air and block sunlight, leading to global cooling. On the other hand, sulfur gases, CO_2, and water vapor are greenhouse gases that cause global warming. **Mass extinctions** are possible results of asteroid impacts or flood basalt eruptions.

CLIMATE AND WEATHER OSCILLATIONS

Natural climate variations take place on time scales of years or decades and are caused by shifts in atmospheric and oceanic conditions. These shifts are due, at least partially, to the way the oceans store and trans- port heat. An example of a natural climate variation is the **El Niño- Southern Oscillation (ENSO)**. ENSO oscillations have a cycle of about 3 to 8 years and are directly related to the interactions between the ocean and atmosphere. ENSO is the foremost source of multiyear variability in weather and climate around the world.

ENSO impacts the South Pacific gyre. In a normal year, the cold Peru Current travels northward up South America. The cold, dense current allows nutrient-rich deep ocean water to rise to the surface, causing plants and animals to thrive. This current travels north to the equator, where the trade winds then push it westward. The equatorial Sun warms the current as it goes. After reaching the western Pacific, most of the water moves north, south, or even back across the equatorial region as a subsurface countercurrent. But some of the water piles up in the western Pacific and continues to warm. The trade winds move from east to west across the equator because the cold water in the eastern equatorial Pacific cools the air above it and creates a low-pressure cell, and the warm water in the western Pacific warms the air above it and creates a high-pressure cell.

In time, the high and low atmospheric pressure cells weaken, causing the trade winds to weaken or reverse direction. These reversed trade winds drag warm water rapidly from west to east, enhancing the countercurrent. When the warm water hits South America, it spreads over the cooler, denser water and shuts off the rising of the deep, nutrient-rich water from below. This begins an **El Niño**, named for the Christ child by Spanish fishermen because the phenomenon often begins around Christmas. Without nutrient-rich water reaching the surface, the marine food web suffers.

An El Niño event ends when most of the warm western Pacific waters have moved east, about one to two years after it begins. When the event is over, normal circulation patterns resume in both the atmosphere and ocean. The oscillation between atmospheric high- and low-pressure cells in the western and eastern Pacific is termed the **Southern Oscillation**. Sometimes, after the El Niño ends, the air and water move to the west more vigorously than normal, and unusually cold water accumulates in the eastern Pacific. This pattern is called **La Niña**.

The change in wind and ocean circulation alters weather patterns worldwide, with some regions experiencing drought while others experience flooding. The Southern Hemisphere is the most affected. Storm activity increases in some locations. Atlantic basin **hurricane** activity decreases during El Niño events and increases during La Niña events. (A hurricane is a potentially deadly tropical storm with high winds, abundant rain, and high seas.)

The North Atlantic Oscillation (NAO) is much weaker than an ENSO, although the patterns are similar. This climate pattern mostly affects Europe. The NAO oscillates between a low-pressure cell over Iceland and a high-pressure cell over the mid-Atlantic Azores Islands. At high NAO, storm tracks are shifted northward into northwestern Europe so that northern Europe is warm and wet, and Mediterranean Europe is dry. At low NAO, storm tracks are shifted southward into the Mediterranean region. Over the past 30 years, the NAO has become more intense, perhaps due to global temperature increases or natural variability.

Pacific climate oscillations also include the Pacific Decadal Oscillation (PDO), with has a 23-year pattern, and the Interdecadal Pacific Oscillation (IPO), which has a 15- to 30- year cycle. Oscillations in the Atlantic include the Atlantic Multidecadal Oscillation (AMO).

WRAP-UP

Natural processes alter Earth's climate on various time scales. Climate can be altered by singular events, such as volcanic eruptions and asteroid impacts. Climate can be altered by short-lived variations in atmosphere-ocean interactions, such as ENSO and NAO, that act on cycles of several years. Milankovitch cycles, which involve the relationship between the Earth's wobble, its tilt, and orbital position relative to the Sun, take place over tens of thousands of years. Large or rapid changes in climate can cause the extinction of species, sometimes even on a mass scale. After a mass extinction, the Earth's ecosystems are very different from the way they were before.

Human Causes
of Climate Change

Human activities increase greenhouse gas levels in the atmosphere. Adding greenhouse gases to the atmosphere is like throwing another blanket on the Earth. The dominant man-made source of greenhouse gases is the burning of fossil fuels and **biomass** (living matter). This chapter also discusses other human activities that alter Earth's climate, including **deforestation** (the removal of trees), **urbanization** (the replacement of natural surfaces with impermeable man-made surfaces), and air pollution.

GREENHOUSE GASES

Like natural processes, human activities remove carbon from reservoirs where it has long been sequestered and send it into the atmosphere. Fossil fuel burning, the most dominant among these activities, releases CO_2 that had been stored in the Earth for millions of years. Burning rain forest to create agricultural or ranch lands, a technique known as **slash-and-burn agriculture** that occurs in the tropics, releases the

CO_2 stored in forests. Deforestation also decreases the amount of CO_2 that is absorbed from the atmosphere by plants. Other types of vegetation, such as crops and grassland, are much less efficient at removing CO_2 from the atmosphere.

Like CO_2 levels, methane levels have been rising precipitously for the past century as human populations have exploded. About 60% of the methane that enters the atmosphere now comes from human activities. Rice production, which feeds a large percentage of the Earth's people, contributes the largest share of methane production. Another source, the gas passed by farm animals, may seem laughable, but its impact is highly significant due to the enormous increases in meat production in recent decades. Storing liquid manure in tanks at massive livestock factory farms causes more methane to enter the atmosphere (although dry manure sitting in a field does not). Methane also comes from decomposition in landfills, waste treatment, and the incomplete burning of rain forest materials.

Other greenhouse gas levels are also increasing because of human activities. Concentrations of ozone in the troposphere, where it is a pollutant and greenhouse gas, have more than doubled since 1976. Tropospheric ozone is created by the action of sunlight on nitrogen oxide and **hydrocarbon** pollutants such as the carbon- and hydrogen-based emissions from car exhaust. Nitrous oxides (NO and N_2O) are themselves greenhouse gases that come from the burning of fossil fuels, forests, and crop wastes, and also from the manufacture and use of fertilizers.

Chlorofluorocarbons (CFCs) are extremely potent greenhouse gases in the troposphere. They also destroy the ozone layer in the stratosphere. CFCs are primarily responsible for the springtime **ozone hole** over Antarctica. Although CFCs were once widely used, production peaked in 1986, and the chemicals are now being phased out. Nevertheless, they will continue to act as greenhouse gases for several decades until solar radiation breaks them down in the atmosphere. Their current substitutes, HFCs, are also greenhouse gases, but they have less heat-trapping ability. Sulfur hexachloride (SF_6) is an extremely potent greenhouse gas that is manufactured for industrial uses.

LAND USE CHANGES

When people change the way they use the land, they may inadvertently alter their climate. The most dramatic example of this is the **urban heat island effect**, the phenomenon whereby urban areas are hotter than the surrounding countryside during the day and especially at night. There are two causes of urban heat island effect: The first is excess heat generated by the running of engines and given off by buildings, among many other sources. The second is the lower albedo of man-made surfaces, such as concrete and asphalt, when compared to natural surfaces. Man-made surfaces store the solar energy that strikes during the day and rerelease it into the atmosphere at night. This is why nighttime temperatures over cities have risen dramatically in the past few decades. For example, in the desert city of Phoenix, Arizona, the nighttime low temperature rose more than 10°F (6.5°C) between 1948 and 2005. The temperature differences between urban areas and the surrounding countryside also make the weather over cities more variable, with more storms and more dry spells.

Land use changes can alter climate in other ways. When forests are converted to farms and ranches, the rates of albedo and evapotranspiration are lower, and the balance of water and heat are thereby altered. Climate patterns are changed: Often the region becomes drier. Urbanization also changes albedo and lowers evaporation in the urbanized area; it reduces precipitation over the city but increases it downwind.

GLOBAL DIMMING

Air pollution influences climate in a number of ways. Particulates from fossil fuel burning are smaller and more abundant than natural particles in the atmosphere. Clouds are made when water vapor condenses around natural particles to form tiny water droplets. The droplets coalesce and, when they become large enough, fall from the sky as rain. Water vapor condenses around pollutant particles, but the particles are too small to coalesce and therefore remain scattered throughout the cloud. A polluted cloud may contain up to six times as many droplets as an unpolluted cloud, thereby reflecting incoming sunlight away from Earth. This phenomenon is called **global dimming**, which brings about a decrease in temperature.

The filtering of incoming solar radiation by polluted clouds has been seen everywhere around the planet. Between the 1950s and the early 1990s, sunlight was reduced 9% in Antarctica, 10% in the United States, 16% in parts of the British Isles, and nearly 30% in Russia. The most extreme reduction was found in Israel, which experienced a 22% decrease in sunlight in a 20-year period that ended in the early 1980s.

Researchers suggest that global dimming has already had dire effects. The horrendous Ethiopian drought that culminated in 1984 and brought about one million deaths and upset 50 million lives, can be explained by global dimming. In Africa, under normal conditions, the summer Sun heats the air north of the equator, generating a low-pressure cell that sucks the summer **monsoon** rains into the Sahel, the semiarid region south of the Sahara desert. (Monsoons bring warm, moist air from the ocean onto the land, often accompanied by intense rains.) The summer monsoon is crucial because it is the only rain that countries in that part of the world, such as Ethiopia, receive. But for twenty years, in the 1970s and 1980s, the monsoon rains did not come into the Sahel.

Global dimming could have been behind this drought. In those decades, large amounts of pollutants from Western Europe and North America wafted over northern Africa, dimming the incoming solar radiation. A large enough dimming could have kept temperatures in the area from increasing enough for the air to rise and suck the monsoon rains northward. With no monsoon rains, the Sahel became drought-stricken.

The Ethiopian drought eventually abated. This can also be explained by global dimming. In the past two decades or more, Western Europe and North America have decreased their pollutant emissions by burning cleaner fuels and installing pollution control devices on smokestacks and exhaust systems. Because of this, fewer pollutants now drift over northern Africa, so the air there heats enough to rise and bring the monsoon rains into the Sahel. Additional pollution

When the Jets Were Grounded

An amazing scientific experiment—one that could not have been performed under any other circumstance—came out of a national tragedy. David Travis of the University of Wisconsin, Whitewater, had been studying the effects of jet plane contrails on climate for 15 years. As shown in the photograph, he could see from satellite photos that contrails sometimes cover as much as 50% to 75% of the sky. He assumed that they had an effect on temperature, but he could not tell what kind and how much. Travis found the opportunity of his research career when, after the terrorist attacks on September 11, 2001, nearly the entire commercial air fleet of the United States was grounded. He knew that by studying the atmosphere in a state that it had never been in during his lifetime—contrail free—he could learn the most about the effects of contrails on climate.

Travis collected data from more than 5,000 weather stations all over the contiguous 48 states. What he discovered was startling: Like clouds, contrails moderate daily temperature swings. Contrails reduce the amount of solar radiation that hits the ground, making days cooler, and trap heat being reemitted from Earth, making nights warmer. During the three-day period in which the planes did not fly, there was an amazing 1.8°F (1°C) increase in temperature across the United States—the great-

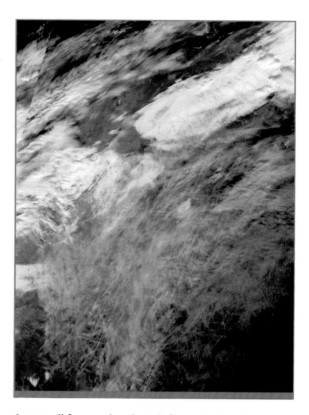

A contrail forms when hot air from a jet engine mixes with cool air in the surrounding environment. Contrails can linger in the sky and over time spread out into thin cloudlike formations. *(NASA /MODIS Rapid Response Team /Goddard Space Flight Center)*

est single temperature effect ever seen. Travis notes that this large effect was due to just one source—other sources of pollutants were not restricted. Therefore, he reasoned, the effect of global dimming from all sources must be huge.

control measures could decrease or end global dimming regionally and globally. But the flip side of a decrease in this pollution could well be an increase in global warming.

WRAP-UP

Human activities are releasing greenhouse gases that have been sequestered in fossil fuels and biomass for millions of years back into the atmosphere. Man-made greenhouse gases such as CFCs that have never before existed on Earth are also being added. Changes in how people use the land—as when they change forests to farmlands or cities—also alter the composition of the atmosphere. Human activities cause climate to cool because atmospheric pollutants block sunlight. Still, scientists have found that global dimming has been counteracting some portion of global warming. As air pollution is reduced, the effect may likely be a further increase in global warming.

John Christy, an atmospheric scientist at the University of Alabama, Huntsville, and a former climate skeptic, stated in a 2004 interview with National Public Radio: "It is scientifically inconceivable that after changing forests into cities, turning millions of acres into farmland, putting massive quantities of soot and dust into the atmosphere and sending quantities of greenhouse gases into the air, that the natural course of climate change hasn't been increased in the past century."

How Scientists Learn About Past, Present, and Future Climate

Earth formed about 4.55 billion years ago, but humans—the genus and species *Homo sapiens*— evolved only about 200,000 years ago. Indeed, nearly all of Earth's past climate occurred before there were people around to witness it. Only during the past millennium have people been chronicling important climatic events, and only in the past century have they kept accurate and consistent weather records. This chapter discusses some of what is known about past climate. Much of this knowledge is the result of the inventive use of the available evidence.

MEASUREMENTS

Meteorology is the study of Earth's atmosphere with the goal of predicting the weather. Since the late 1800s, meteorologists have been measuring weather characteristics such as temperature, precipitation, and wind speed and direction from land-based stations and, more recently, from weather balloons. In 1960, meteorologists began to use satellites to gather weather data. Because satellites see a large and clear picture from high above Earth's surface, they are extremely important for chronicling global climate change. Satellites have gathered decades' worth of information on pollution, fires, ocean temperature, ocean current patterns, ice boundaries, volcanic ash clouds, and many other climate-related features. For example, images gathered each year for two decades detail the loss of ice cover during Arctic summers over that time period.

CLIMATE PROXIES

Paleoclimatologists (**paleoclimatology** is the study of past climate) have developed many innovative techniques for getting information about the history of Earth's climate. These scientists use biological or physical clues, known as **climate proxies**, to unravel past climate patterns over the entire planet or over specific regions. These clues are found in **ice cores**, **tree rings**, and sediments, for example, and can be used to reconstruct past climate with surprising depth and accuracy. Some climate proxies, for example, preserve evidence of past temperatures. Using these proxies, paleoclimatologists have reconstructed Earth's climate history in differing amounts of detail that reach back millions of years.

Unique tools are used for different time scales. Ice cores yield climate data that cover hundreds of thousands of years. Sediments in the ocean floors go back millions of years. **Sedimentary rocks** from the surface of the earth are rocks that are made of sediments or that precipitate from water. These rocks can give general information about climate that goes back billions of years. Although tree ring cores taken from living trees are only useful for as many years as the tree has lived, logs that are preserved by becoming petrified in rock or sediments yield information about time periods that are much further back.

Ice Cores

The most powerful window into past climate is the ice contained in glaciers and ice caps. To collect an ice core, scientists drill a hollow pipe into an ice sheet or glacier. The cores taken from the Greenland

and Antarctic ice caps supply data that span long periods of time: Two Greenland cores go back 100,000 years, while one Antarctic core goes back 420,000 years, through four glacial cycles. The European Project for Ice Coring in Antarctica (EPICA), about two miles (3,190 m) long, has cut through eight glacial cycles covering 740,000 years and is still being drilled. Mountain ice cores are thinner and have much shorter records, but they can be collected from regions scattered around the Earth.

Polar ice caps may contain as many as 100,000 layers of ice. Each layer yields age and weather data from the time when it was deposited. High up in an ice core, close to the surface, each layer represents one year: The age of the sample can be determined simply by counting backwards from the top of the core. Deeper in the core, where the layers have been compacted by overlying ice, only multiple year blocks can be distinguished. To determine the age of a deeper layer, events with known ages that have left evidence of their occurrence in the layer can be identified. Useful recent events are nuclear bomb tests that have left deposits of radioactive **isotopes** in the ice. Volcanic ash is valuable for ice of any age because the ash can be correlated to specific eruptions far back in time. Age can also be determined by the chemistry of marine sediments.

Gases and particles trapped in snowfall can be analyzed by examining ice layers. These substances represent atmospheric conditions at the time the snow fell. Scientists can analyze CO_2 in the gases to determine the concentration of that greenhouse gas at the time and to ascertain its source, whether from volcanic eruptions or burning fossil fuels, for example. The presence of Beryllium-10 in the ice core is evidence of the strength of solar radiation. Ash indicates a volcanic eruption, dust an expansion of deserts, and pollen the types of plants that were on the planet at the time. The amount of pollen found in the ice layer may be an indicator of the amount of precipitation that fell.

Paleoclimatologists can discern air temperature at the time the snow fell by measuring the ratios of different isotopes of oxygen and hydrogen. These isotope ratios also reveal global sea level.

By using isotopes and many other chemical and physical indicators trapped in the ice, scientists can reconstruct atmospheric temperature, ocean volume, precipitation, the composition of the lower atmosphere, volcanic eruptions, solar variability, the productivity of plankton at the sea surface, the extent of deserts, and the presence of forest fires. Most importantly for paleoclimatologists, they can construct a record of climate change through the period of time represented by the core.

Sediments

Sediments collect in layers on seafloors and lake bottoms. Like ice, sediments can be drilled as cores with the oldest layer located at the bottom. Sediments can be found dating back millions of years. They

Isotopes and Their Scientific Uses

An **atom** is the smallest unit of a chemical **element** (a substance that cannot be chemically reduced to simpler substances) having the properties of that element. At an atom's center is its **nucleus**, which contains **protons** that have small, positive electrical charges and **neutrons** that have no charge. An atom's **atomic weight** is the sum of its protons and neutrons. A particular element, for example, potassium, will always have the same number of protons in its nucleus, but it may have a different number of neutrons. Potassium always has 19 protons but it can have 20, 21, or 22 neutrons. Therefore, the atomic weight of a potassium nucleus can be 39, 40, or 41, which creates the different isotopes of potassium: potassium-39, potassium-40, or potassium-41.

Oxygen isotopes are especially important in deciphering Earth's past climate. Nearly all oxygen is either ^{16}O (8 protons and 8 neutrons) or ^{18}O (8 protons and 10 neutrons). Either isotope may become part of a water molecule. H_2O containing ^{16}O is "light" and so is slightly more likely to evaporate than "heavy" H_2O containing ^{18}O. When water evaporates, the water vapor is enriched in ^{16}O while the liquid water left behind is enriched in ^{18}O. Therefore, the $^{18}O/^{16}O$ of the liquid is relatively high, and the $^{18}O/^{16}O$ of the vapor is relatively low. Similarly, a heavy water molecule (one containing ^{18}O) is slightly more likely to condense to form a raindrop or snowflake than

can be composed of sand, rock fragments, clay, dust, ash, preserved vegetation, animal fossils, and pollen.

Perhaps the most useful sediments are the remains of plankton that once floated at the ocean surface before dying and sinking to the bottom. These tiny shells harbor many kinds of information on the conditions of the atmosphere and surrounding seawater. One type of plankton—small, coiled foraminifera (forams)—are extremely sensitive to ocean temperature, and therefore each of the species in this group is present only within a specific, narrow temperature range. The presence of a particular species in a core yields the sea surface temperature (SST) at the time the organisms lived. One species of foram, *Neogloboquadrina pachyderma*, changes its coiling direction from left

a light water molecule. For that reason, the $^{18}O/^{16}O$ of the raindrop is higher than that of the remaining vapor. Hydrogen isotopes work the same way, with lighter ^{1}H (one proton) more likely to be in water vapor and heavier ^{2}H, (one proton and one neutron) more likely to be in liquid water.

Air cools as it rises or moves toward the poles and releases some of its moisture. Because ^{18}O is more likely to condense into a raindrop, the first precipitation to fall has a relatively high $^{18}O/^{16}O$ ratio. With time, the ^{18}O is depleted from the air so the $^{18}O/^{16}O$ ratio of the raindrops decreases. Because air moves toward the poles from the equator, $^{18}O/^{16}O$ decreases with increasing latitude.

As a result of these processes, higher $^{18}O/^{16}O$ indicates warmer air temperatures; lower $^{18}O/^{16}O$ indicates cooler temperatures. Therefore, $^{18}O/^{16}O$ is a proxy for temperature. $^{1}H/^{2}H$ can also be used to reconstruct the temperature at the time of precipitation. These isotopes can be used as a proxy for temperature in ice cores and marine sediments.

As temperature increases and ice sheets melt, fresh water enriched in light oxygen returns to the sea. Low $^{18}O/^{16}O$ ratios indicate less ice cover and, therefore, higher temperatures. $^{18}O/^{16}O$ is also a proxy for local rainfall: Because the ^{18}O precipitates first, low $^{18}O/^{16}O$ means that a large amount of rain has already fallen.

to right when the surface water temperature warms above 46°F (8°C). With temperature information from all around the seafloor, scientists can reconstruct the patterns of ocean currents during any time period from the past 150 million years or more.

The isotope ratios of marine fossils also contain useful information. $^{18}O/^{16}O$ in shells, teeth, bone, and other hard tissues yield the temperature at the time the organism lived. The shells of some forams contain an average of 2% more ^{18}O during a glacial period than a warm period. $^{18}O/^{16}O$ can also be used to calculate the amount of the Earth that was covered by ice. Because heavy water is more likely to precipitate near the equator, snow that falls in the high latitudes is light. During an ice age, this light snow is trapped in ice sheets, and therefore seawater is enriched in ^{18}O. The $^{18}O/^{16}O$ value of seawater is therefore directly related to the amount of ^{16}O-enriched ice that covers the Earth. Oxygen isotopes also give information on sea level: A rise or fall in $^{18}O/^{16}O$ of just 0.01% indicates a 33 foot (10 m) change in sea level.

Sedimentary Rock

Sedimentary rock does not give as detailed a picture of past climate as ice cores and marine or lake sediments. Sedimentary rocks' value is that they are widespread and are available from much further back in Earth history, even going back hundreds of millions of years. Sedimentary rocks contain the only remaining paleoclimate information for much of Earth history.

Many sedimentary rocks can only be deposited in a restricted range of climates. Modern coral reefs, for example, only grow in the tropics; therefore, fossil reefs indicate that the region was tropical at the time the coral reef grew. Rock that was formed from glacial deposits indicates a cold climate, while coal was formed in a warm and wet environment. Limestone forms in warm shallow seas. The ratio of $^{18}O/^{16}O$ in sedimentary rocks indicates how much rain was falling when the rocks were deposited and where the moisture may have come from. Scientists can use these data to reconstruct atmospheric circulation patterns.

Tree Rings

Each year a tree grows a new layer of wood under the bark. This creates a tree ring, which varies in size depending on the temperature and precipitation conditions at the time of growth. Narrow rings are from cool, dry years and wider rings represent warm, wet years. Tree rings are useful only in locations where there is an annual seasonal cycle of temperature and precipitation, such as in the temperate zones.

Trees do not live more than a few centuries, but evidence of past climate can be reconstructed from logs found in ice, permafrost, or glacial sediments. Tree ring data from petrified trees can yield information from much further back in time. The age of these trees can be determined using radiocarbon dating, which measures the abundance of carbon isotopes that undergo radioactive decay at a known rate.

CLIMATE MODELS

Scientists input the information gathered from modern measurements, paleoclimate data, and current ideas on how land, atmosphere, oceans, and ice interact into a supercomputer to construct **climate models**. A climate model can be created for a local area or for the entire Earth.

Climate is very complex, and climate models are difficult to construct. Many aspects of climate are not well understood. Simple climate models look at a single atmospheric characteristic and its effect on a single condition, such as the effect of rising carbon dioxide levels on surface air temperatures. Simple models can be combined to generate more complex models. For example, the effect of rising temperature on separate layers of the atmosphere can be combined into a model of the changes in temperature and circulation expected for the entire atmosphere. The more factors that are put into the model, the more complex it is, and the less certainty scientists may have regarding the accuracy of the outcome.

To check the validity of a new model, scientists try to replicate events that have already occurred. For example, they might construct a model to predict the effect of increased air temperature on sea surface temperature (SST) since 1980. They begin with air and ocean temperatures from 1980 and then input the increased air temperatures measured since that time. The scientists then run the model to see whether it correctly predicts current SST. If it does, the model can then be used to predict the future with some degree of confidence. Models are also continuously updated.

The success of a model depends in part on the scientists' ability to account for the interactions of land, atmosphere, ocean, and living things. Yet, some factors are not well understood. Clouds, for example, have two competing effects on climate: They reflect sunlight back into space (as when a cloud passes overhead) and they trap heat (as on a cloudy night). If warmer temperatures increase cloud cover, the effects are unclear and so are not easy to model.

Models must take into account **feedback mechanisms**, situations in which a small change in something in the system magnifies the original effect and therefore causes a much greater effect. Feedback mechanisms can go in either direction: With a **positive feedback mechanism**, one action leads to a set of events that increase that action. For example, as the Earth warms, water evaporates, which increases the amount of water vapor in the atmosphere. Because water vapor is a greenhouse gas, air temperature increases even more. The increase causes more water to evaporate and consequently causes air temperature to rise.

With a **negative feedback mechanism**, one action leads to a set of events that weaken that action. For example, as the temperature warms, more water vapor in the atmosphere causes more clouds to form. Low clouds reflect a large percentage of incoming sunlight, which slows warming. This would be an example of negative feedback.

Positive and negative feedback mechanisms show the complexity of the climate system. A partial list of feedback mechanisms that result from warmer temperatures is shown in the table on page 47.

Threshold effects are also important when modeling climate. An example of a threshold effect is that a rise in temperature of 1.8°F (1°C) from 29.3° to 31.1°F (-1.5° to -0.5°C) will not have much effect on a local glacier. However, the same magnitude of temperature increase

Some Positive and Negative Feedbacks from Warming Temperatures

POSITIVE FEEDBACK MECHANISMS	NEGATIVE FEEDBACK MECHANISMS
Transition of snow and ice to water and plants decreases albedo.	Increased pollution, emitted from same sources as greenhouse gases, reflects sunlight.
Melting permafrost releases methane and other hydrocarbon greenhouse gases into the atmosphere.	Increased CO_2 stimulates plant growth, which absorbs atmospheric CO_2.
Increasing greenhouse gases	Increased cloud cover reflects sunlight, cooling the atmosphere and surface.
Increased cloud cover: Clouds absorb heat radiating from Earth's surface.	Warmer winter temperatures cause people to use less heat, so less fossil fuel is burned.
Breakdown of carbonates releases CO_2.	
Oceans warm and release CO_2.	
Water warms and atmospheric water vapor increases.	
Warmer summer temperatures stimulate the use of more air conditioning, which uses more fossil fuels.	
Warmer spring and summer temperatures instigate more wildfires, which burn trees, releasing their carbon into the atmosphere.	
Warmer temperatures bring on drought, which reduces plant growth and reduces the amount of CO_2 the plants take in.	

will have an enormous effect if the rise is from 31.1° to 32.9°F (−0.5° to 0.5°C) because that temperature increase crosses the threshold for ice to melt. Important temperature thresholds are different for specific locations, for biological systems, and for the planet as a whole.

WRAP-UP

Scientists have developed ingenious ways to reconstruct Earth's climate history. Using a wide variety of techniques, paleoclimatologists can know something of the climate of the far distant past and much more about the climate of the more recent past. Ice cores are the most valuable tool and allow scientists to understand the climate on timescales of up to hundreds of thousands of years. Ocean sediments reveal similar data for timescales of up to tens of millions of years. Sedimentary rocks yield climate secrets from even further back. Local climate information can be determined using many other techniques, such as tree rings. After scientists compile all of the relevant climate information, they create climate models that describe the past and attempt to predict the future. Some of what these scientists have learned about past climate will be discussed in the following chapter.

Climate Change Through Earth History

Constructing a history of Earth's climate is easiest when examining more recent time periods because there are more tools available and better recordkeeping. Nonetheless, climatologists have been able to construct a detailed record of the planet's more distant climate history, going back thousands of years. This chapter discusses how climate has played an important role in the evolution of life and has even guided the course of human history.

ANCIENT CLIMATE

During much of Earth's history, the planet has been relatively warm and wet, with no glaciers or ice sheets. These steamy periods were punctuated by ice ages, when much of the planet's surface was coated in ice. On average, over Earth's history, the planet's temperature was between 14°F and 27°F (8°C and 15°C) warmer than the temperature today. Scientists speculate that a temperature variance of only 18°F (10°C) makes the difference between a fully glacial earth and an ice-free planet, in part because high temperatures are more extreme at high latitudes where the presence or absence of ice sheets play an important role in global climate. Conditions now are relatively cool because the planet is coming off the extreme cold of the Pleistocene Ice Ages, which ended about 10,000 years ago.

Atmospheric greenhouse gas concentrations have also varied in Earth history. CO_2 has fluctuated from between less than 200 ppm to greater than 5,000 ppm, a high concentration reached hundreds of millions of years ago. Ice core and other samples show that greenhouse gas levels correlate with temperatures: When CO_2 or methane levels are high, temperatures are also high.

PALEOCENE-EOCENE THERMAL MAXIMUM

After the mass extinctions at the end of the Cretaceous Period, 65 million years ago, the planet was relatively warm and ice free. Temperatures rose until they became so high they triggered an even greater warming event around 55 million years ago. This period is known as the **Paleocene-Eocene Thermal Maximum (PETM)**, a time when the Arctic was swampy and Antarctica was covered with forests.

Paleoclimatologists are piecing together the story of the PETM, mostly from the chemistry of forams collected from ocean sediment cores. The PETM arose over a very short period of time geologically. About half of the warming, 3.6°F (2°C), took place over no more than a few hundred years, with the rest occurring over less than 5,000 years. Sea surface temperatures increased by between 9° and 14°F (5° and 8°C), with a striking rise of 15°F (8.3°C) occurring in the polar regions. The deep sea warmed dramatically as well.

Forams show a major decline in the ratio of heavy carbon (^{13}C) to light carbon (^{12}C) across the Paleocene-Eocene boundary. The explanation favored by scientists is that a load of methane, which is rich in light carbon, flooded the atmosphere. The most likely source of such vast amounts of methane is the methane hydrate deposits buried in seafloor sediments. According to this scenario, the PETM was triggered when ocean temperatures rose above a critical threshold: the temperature at which methane hydrates melt. Melting released the methane trapped inside the hydrates, and the greenhouse gas deluged the atmosphere. Such large increases in atmospheric methane explain the rapid and extreme global warming seen during the PETM.

The high temperatures of the PETM had many consequences. Warm surface waters caused ocean currents to switch direction, a condition that lasted for about 20,000 years. Because warm water cannot hold as much gas as cold water, oceanic oxygen levels were very low. In the atmosphere, methane broke down and formed CO_2, which then formed carbonic acid. The evidence for this is that the deep ocean sediments are very rich in clays, suggesting that the carbonate shells of many organisms dissolved. High acidity and low oxygen caused 50% of deep sea forams and possibly other deep sea animals to die out. While there was no mass extinction on land or in the surface ocean, fossil evidence supports changes in the abundance of some life forms and in their evolutionary pathways. This is the time when modern mammals, from rodents to primates, first evolved and flourished. The PETM lasted for about 200,000 years, likely ending when all the available methane had been released into the atmosphere. Over time, the CO_2 that the methane broke down into was sequestered in forests and plankton and dissolved into the oceans.

THE PLEISTOCENE ICE AGES

After the end of the PETM, temperatures fell, ultimately bottoming out during the Pleistocene Ice Ages, which began 1.8 million years ago and ended 10,000 years ago. The Pleistocene was not a time of relentless cold: Glaciers advanced and retreated many times. At the height of the most recent glacial advance, between 18,000 and 22,000 years ago, glaciers covered much of Eurasia and North America, from New York City northward. Average global temperatures were about 10°F (5.5°C) colder, and sea level was about 395 feet (125 m) lower than today. The low sea level exposed the Bering land bridge, allowing humans and large animals to migrate from Asia into North America. The bountiful forests south of the ice sheets were home to giant ice age mammals such as cave bears, saber-toothed cats, and wooly mammoths.

During the warm periods, known as interglacials, temperatures were more than 2°F (1.1°C) higher, and sea level was about 16 feet (4.8 m) higher than today. CO_2 was higher than during the glacial periods but never rose above 300 ppm. Interglacial periods lasted about 10,000 years (although one of them lasted as long as 27,000 years). Even the interglacial periods were broken up by relatively short cold spells. CO_2 was stable at or below 280 ppm for at least 400,000 years.

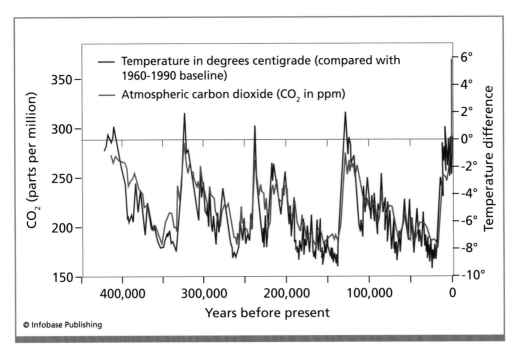

© Infobase Publishing

CO_2 and temperature show the same pattern in the Vostok ice core from Antarctica over the past 400,000 years. Temperature and CO_2 are high during interglacial periods and low during glacial periods. CO_2 does not drive the initial rise in temperature during an interglacial, but it is a major contributor later. The rise in CO_2 since 1958 has been picked up by the Mauna Loa monitoring station; temperature has not kept up with CO_2.

The glacials and interglacials of the Pleistocene were caused by the Milankovitch and other natural cycles. Greenhouse gas levels also played a role. At the beginning of each glacial advance, CO_2 and methane plunged and then resurged at the end. Ice cores from Greenland and Antarctica exhibit CO_2 values that are 30% lower during glacial periods than during interglacial periods.

Climate changed quickly during the Pleistocene, with rapid transitions between glacial and interglacial periods. One especially dramatic temperature change took place early in the interglacial period that began 12,700 years ago. At about 10,500 years ago, as glaciers were retreating, the warming trend suddenly reversed. Temperatures in parts of the Northern Hemisphere fell as much as 20°F (11°C) in as little as 10 to 100 years. The summit of Greenland was 27°F (15°C) colder, and Great Britain was 9°F (5°C) colder than they are now. This climatic period, which lasted about 1,400 years, is called the Younger Dryas. At the end of the Younger Dryas, temperatures returned to normal in only about 10 years.

Such rapid and dramatic cooling was likely the result of a massive influx of freshwater from North America. When an enormous lake of glacial melt water that was held back by an ice dam was breached, freshwater flooded the North Atlantic. The freshwater was light and floated on the sea surface, shutting down thermohaline circulation. As a result, warm equatorial waters were stopped from flowing northward.

CLIMATE CHANGE IN HUMAN HISTORY

In the past 10,000 years, since the end of the Pleistocene Ice Ages, average global temperature has risen 7°F (4°C). Glaciers have been in retreat since then and are now found only in high mountains and at high latitudes. Despite ups and downs, climate over the past 10 millennia has been milder and more stable than at any time since the Emiam interglacial of 130,000 years ago. Perhaps not surprisingly, this favorable climate period is the one during which human civilization developed. In his 2006 book, *The Winds of Change: Climate,*

Weather, and the Destruction of Civilizations, Eugene Linden connects climate change with the rise and fall of civilizations. Linden cites scientists who say that climate does not shift from consistently warm to consistently cold but flickers rapidly between warm and cold and wet and dry over several decades. "Rapid shifts between warm and cold throw ecosystems out of balance, unleashing pests and microbes, and ruining crops," says Linden. Just a few of the fascinating scenarios he presents, linking climatic shifts with cultural development, are presented below.

The generally upward temperature trend since the end of the Pleistocene has been punctuated by periods of more rapid warming and of rapid cooling. The most severe cooling was a freshwater influx into the North Atlantic around 8,200 years ago that caused a plunge in temperatures of 9°F (5°C). This event was similar to the Younger Dryas but lasted between 60 and 200 years. This cooling event interrupted the emergence of civilization in Turkey, where agriculture and cities had been developing. The return of cold, dry, and windy weather necessitated that people devote their energy not to innovation but to survival.

Ice core data show that the period from 8,000 to 5,200 years ago was relatively warm, allowing the development of irrigated agriculture and permanent settlements. An abrupt cooling that occurred about 5,200 years ago again derailed cultural advances. Conditions were very cold and very wet, although this period seems to correspond with the beginning of cities in Mesopotamia and the Nile Valley and with the start of calendars.

Climate again stabilized, and the Bronze Age began, although at different times in different parts of Europe and the Middle East. This stable climatic period was the time of the Akkadian empire, which emerged around the city of Akkad in Ancient Mesopotamia, beginning about 4,350 years ago. The Akkadians had a written language, an accounting system, and religious practices that suggest a sophisticated social organization. A heavy dust band in ice cores on Mount Huascarán in Peru and on Mount Kilimanjaro in Africa provides evidence of a disastrous drought that brought on massive starvation and brought an abrupt end in to the Akkadian Empire 4,200 years ago. The dust band was discovered by Professor Lonnie Thompson of

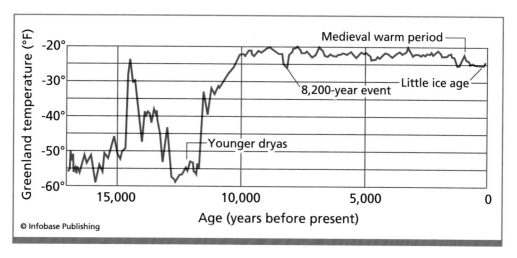

Scientists have uncovered the temperatures over the Greenland ice sheet for the past 18,000 years. This plot shows the very large plunge into the Younger Dryas, the much smaller dip at 8,200 years, and the relatively tiny ups and downs of the Medieval Warm Period and Little Ice Age. The most recent temperatures do not show up on the graph.

the Byrd Polar Research Center of Ohio State University. Global patterns of droughts and flooding from that time period suggest that the climate was dominated by an extremely strong El Niño that lasted for more than two centuries.

Climate sometimes wreaks destruction on humans (or organisms) by creating the conditions that promote the spread of disease. The Justinian Plague, which occurred in A.D. 541 to 542, was the first **pandemic**, an outbreak of infectious disease that spreads over a large region of the world. This plague may have originated in a rapid freeze that came in A.D. 536. No one knows what caused temperatures to plummet, but the rapid change indicates that the event was catastrophic, such as an asteroid impact. The cold snap brought on a cycle of floods and drought, which increased the food supply for East African rodents and caused their populations to increase faster than their predators' populations. The rodents harbored fleas (*Xenopsylla cheopis*) that contained the bubonic plague bacterium *Yersinia pestis*. The rodents are not susceptible to the disease, but the plague bacteria block the fleas' digestive tracts. The fleas bite everything to try to slake their hunger, spreading the infection as they go. The plague bacteria migrated northward on fleas that eventually infected *Rattus rattus*, the black rat, which has lived in close proximity with humans for millennia. The Justinian Plague laid waste to Constantinople, Alexandria, and other major world cities, killing millions of people during the following two centuries.

Lonnie Thompson: Constructing Earth's Climate from the World's High Peaks

Lonnie Thompson's life began far from the tropical mountain peaks where he now spends much of his time. As a boy on a farm in rural West Virginia, he was fascinated with meteorology. He attended Marshall College, where he studied to become a coal geologist. Thompson married the only woman studying physics at Marshall, Ellen Mosely, and the couple moved to Ohio State University for graduate school. Thompson's life took a fateful turn when he secured a research job working with the first ice cores ever collected. The young geologist was entranced by the immense possibilities that ice cores held for the reconstruction of past climate and was inspired to switch his studies to glaciology. After one field season in Antarctica, Thompson decided to study tropical mountain glaciers, ignoring the prevailing idea that mountain glaciers were too active to contain a usable climate history. In 1974, he became the first scientist to drill a mountain glacier, the Quelccaya ice cap, at an elevation of 18,600 feet (5,670 m) in the Peruvian Andes, and he has worked on mountain glaciers ever since.

Gathering ice on tropical mountain glaciers presents unique difficulties. Tropical mountain glaciers are at very high altitudes. At those heights, people are susceptible to acute mountain sickness, pulmonary edema, frostbite, and other ills, all of which have plagued members of Thompson's ice coring team. The sample sites are inaccessible to aircraft and other vehicles, so people (sometimes with the help of yaks) must maneuver six tons (5.4 metric tons) of equipment over the jagged and crevassed glacial surface, while avoiding avalanches, altitude sickness, frigid temperatures, and windstorms. Cores are retrieved in one-meter sections and stored in insulated boxes. When drilling is complete, about four tons (3.6 metric tons) of cores must be quickly carried down the mountain, transported overland, and then placed aboard an airplane. These cores must be shipped to the OSU center before they melt. Once they

The **Medieval Warm Period (MWP)** lasted from about A.D. 900 to 1300. Although its cause is not yet well understood, it seems to be related to a strengthening of Atlantic meridional overturning. The MWP was a time of relatively warm, dry temperatures (although it is worth noting that temperatures during the MWP were never as high as during the 1990s). In Europe, crops thrived, and the people were

reach the research center, they are stored in refrigerated vaults that are maintained at Arctic temperatures of -22°F (-30°C).

Thompson braves these adverse conditions because of the important story that tropical mountain glaciers have to tell about regional climate and environmental change. Tropical glaciers contain a thorough record of El Niño events and, he says, understanding the natural variability of these natural climate events is essential for assessing the degree to which human activities are now inducing climate change. Tropical regions are also extremely sensitive to greenhouse gas levels: If rising CO_2 causes tropical oceans to evaporate, the added water vapor will raise atmospheric greenhouse gas levels even higher and increase global temperatures.

Thompson is now the world's foremost expert in the study of paleoclimate using ice cores from mountain glaciers. Over the past 30 years, he has led more than 50 expeditions to 11 high-elevation ice fields on 5 continents. He has cored about 23,000 feet (7,000 m) of ice reaching as far back in time as 750,000 years. The scientist is now in a race against time to gather as many ice cores as he can before the ice record melts away. He estimates that the Peruvian Andes, which contain the world's largest concentration of tropical glaciers, have lost about 20% of their mass since 1972. For example, in the years 1991–2005, Qori Kalis glacier retreated about 10 times faster (200 feet [61 m] per year) than during the years from 1963 to 1978 (20 feet [6.1 m] per year).

As Thompson stated in *Ohio State Research* in 2006, "What this [research] is really telling us is that our climate system is sensitive, it can change abruptly due to either natural or to human forces. If what happened 5,000 years ago were to happen today, it would have far-reaching social and economic implications for the entire planet. The take-home message is that global climate can change abruptly, and with 6.5 billion people inhabiting the planet, that's serious."

healthy and prosperous. Europe's population quadrupled, and life expectancy increased to about 48 years of age. These favorable conditions allowed people to focus on art and religion, erecting extraordinary cathedrals and castles.

MWP climate was not nearly as advantageous in western North America and Central America: That part of the world suffered near-permanent drought. The Maya civilization, centered in the Yucatan Peninsula of Mexico and the highlands of Guatemala, was in full swing when the drought began. Over a period of about 1,200 years,

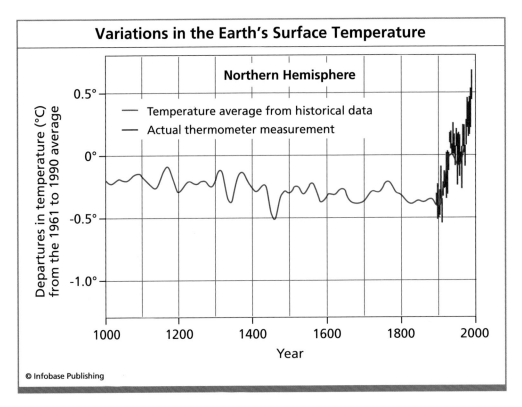

Variations in the Earth's Surface Temperature

© Infobase Publishing

Temperature for the past 1,000 years from tree rings, ice cores, historical records, and thermometers shows a large rise in recent years. At no time in this graph does temperature rise above the 1961 to 1990 average (shown as the zero line) until the past few decades. The Medieval Warm Period (900–1300) shows much lower average temperatures than seen in the recent warming trend.

the Maya had built a remarkable civilization. They had constructed glorious pyramids, such as those located at Chichen Itza and Tikal. The Maya were advanced in astronomy, the calendar, and in a skill that was extremely important for their drought-prone location: water management. Mayan farmers depended on annual rains from late spring to early fall for maize production, and on their rulers for drinking and household water during the annual dry season. Water was the means by which the Mayan elite maintained their rule because only they had the resources to store water in reservoirs and maintain its quality.

Temple of the Jaguar at the Tikal Mayan archaeological park, Guatemala. (*hroldan, iStock International, Inc.*)

Despite its accomplishments, the Mayan civilization collapsed around A.D. 900. Many hypotheses have been offered, but new seafloor sediment analyses and tree ring data point to extreme drought as the primary cause. Because reservoirs could store water only for a year or two, when Mayan rulers were no longer able to supply their subjects with water, the civilization failed. Farmers moved to other areas or, more likely, died of starvation and thirst. People weakened by famine are also more prone to disease.

The MWP was far kinder to the Vikings (Norse), who spread across the northern portion of Europe. The Norse had thriving colonies on Greenland and on Iceland, where they grew crops, raised farm animals, and hunted. But in the fourteenth century, Europe plunged into the Little Ice Age (LIA), which ebbed and flowed over the next 500 years, though scientists debate the exact dates of this period. This temperature drop came at somewhat different times in different locations: It struck Greenland in 1343. Archaeological evidence shows that at least one household slowly starved over the years until the inhabitants finally died out in 1355, the worst winter in 500 years.

During the LIA, global temperatures dropped between 0.9°F and 1.8°F (0.5°C and 1.0°C), a minor amount compared to those frigid periods of early civilization discussed on pages 53–56. Because the LIA was likely caused by a slowing of Atlantic meridional overturning, the largest temperature change was in the North Atlantic region, where the average temperature dropped 5.4°F (3°C). In Europe, weather during the LIA was often frigid, but it could also be warm, stormy, or dry in any combination. The extremely variable weather

European painters captured images of life during the Little Ice Age. This undated watercolor by Hendrick Avercamp (1585 to 1663) is entitled "Life on Ice at Sunset in Amsterdam." *(Bildarchiv Preussischer Kulturbesitz /Art Resource, NY)*

led to failed crops. Famine killed millions of people and triggered social conflict and war.

The LIA struck Great Britain earlier than Greenland. The River Thames, which flows through London, froze in 1309, but then the weather warmed up and brought in large storms. Crops rotted or failed to ripen, and livestock froze. Beginning in 1332, the cycle of floods and drought in Mongolia and China brought about the bubonic plague. After killing 35 million people in China, the Black Death spread to Europe, where it killed between one-quarter and one-half of the population: 20 to 50 million people who were already weakened by famine and other diseases. Bubonic plague came and went over the next few centuries.

Still, the LIA was not a time of constant cold: Between 1400 and 1550, the climate became more moderate. This mild period correlates with the Renaissance, a time of great technological and artistic advances. Then, from 1550 to 1850, winters again turned long and severe, and summers were short and wet. In the seventeenth century, in Switzerland, glaciers advanced down mountain valleys and crushed villages. In North America, in the winter of 1780, New York Harbor froze solid, allowing people to walk from Manhattan to Staten Island.

Superimposed on the LIA was the Maunder Minimum, a period with extremely low sunspot activity. This period corresponds with the deepest cold of the LIA, from 1645 to 1715.

WRAP-UP

Scientists can learn about many important things from studying past climate. Evidence from ice cores, ocean sediments, and other sources has shown paleoclimatologists that climate change was not always gradual and sometimes was extremely rapid. As climate changes from hot to cold or cold to hot, it does not do so abruptly, but flickers between the two states. Periods of great climatic change have generally been difficult during human history. Times such as the MWP and the LIA took enormous tolls on civilizations: Famine, thirst, and disease sometimes caused the deaths of tens of millions of people.

Climate Now

The relatively mild weather of the past two millennia aided the development of human civilization. The byproduct of that development has been the rapid rise of greenhouse gas emissions in the past one and a half centuries. This chapter explores climate change in recent times, particularly in the past few decades, during which the climatic effects of those emissions have been very apparent.

RECENT CLIMATE

Over the past 10,000 years, global temperature rose 7°F (4°C). And one-seventh of that temperature rise, 1°F (0.6°C), occurred within a period of only 100 years: between 1900 and 2000. The twentieth century temperature rise was not uniform over time. Temperatures rose for the first 40 years, and then decreased slightly over the next 25. However, since the early 1970s, temperatures have risen abruptly, with an increase of about 0.7°F (0.4°C), including a major upswing beginning in 1990.

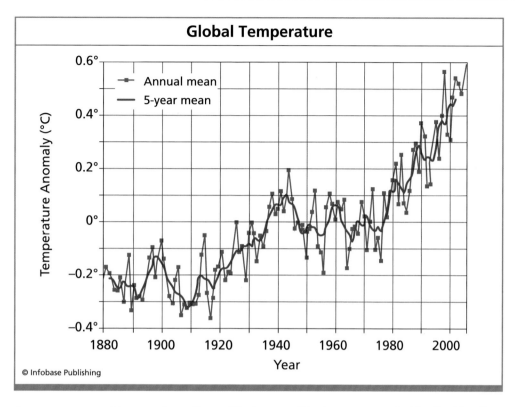

Average measured temperatures from 1880 to 2005. The boxes connected by the blue line show the annual mean measured temperature. The red line is the 5-year mean. The zero line is the 1961 to 1990 average temperature.

The graph of temperatures over the past 1,000 years is known as "the hockey stick graph," a name that at least somewhat describes its shape (see the figure on page 58). The graph shows greater rise in temperature and higher temperatures in the past two decades than at any time, including the Medieval Warm Period (MWP). This finding is supported by a 2006 report of the U.S. National Academy of Sciences. Recent scientific evidence shows that the past 10- to 20-year period was the warmest period of at least the past two millennia.

A look at average global temperatures from the time record-keeping began in 1880 through 2006 shows that the 12 hottest years occurred

The Hottest Years on Record

RANK	YEAR	RANK	YEAR	RANK	YEAR	RANK	YEAR
1	2005	6	2004	11	1999	16	1994
2	1998	7	2001	12	2000	17	1983
3	2002	8	1997	13	1991	18	1996
4	2003	9	1990	14	1987	19	1944
5	2006	10	1995	15	1988	20	1989

Source: National Aeronautic and Space Administration (NASA)

since 1990. Indeed, every year since 1994 is on the list of 20, and only one of the top 20 hottest years was before 1983 (1944, at number 19).

Temperatures have increased in both summer and winter. July 2006 was the second hottest July ever recorded in the United States, through 2006. (The previous hottest July temperatures occurred in 1936, at the peak of the Dust Bowl.) The average global temperature of 77.2°F (25.1°C) for July 2006 was just slightly lower than the July record average temperature of 77.5°F (25.3°C) and much higher than the historical average of 74.3°F (23.5°C). About 2,300 records were set for daily high temperatures and 3,200 for highest low temperatures. Europe also experienced a heat wave, and the Netherlands, Belgium, Ireland, and the United Kingdom had their hottest July ever.

The following winter, from December 2006 through February 2007, was the warmest winter on record worldwide, although temperatures were near normal in the United States. The winter from December 2005 to February 2006 was one of the warmest ever in the United States, and January 2006 was the warmest of that month on record. The reason temperatures were so high that January was because of the jet stream. (The jet stream is a stream of air high in the atmosphere that separates cold temperatures in the north from warm temperatures in the south.) Ordinarily, if temperatures are unusually warm in one location, they are unusually cold in another, depending on the location of the jet stream. But that month the jet stream was extremely far north, so warm temperatures prevailed all over North America.

Recent rising temperatures have not been spread evenly around the Earth. The high latitudes have warmed most dramatically. In the past two decades, temperatures have risen as much as 8°F (4.4°C) in some Arctic locations. Some industrialized countries, such as the United States, have warmed less than the rest of the world, probably due to global dimming. While most locations have warmed, a few, such as the North Atlantic Ocean, have cooled.

Warmer temperatures have increased precipitation overall, but not uniformly. Average precipitation over the land has increased by about 2% since 1900. The mid and high latitudes over the Northern Hemisphere have experienced an increase in precipitation of 0.5 to 1.0% per decade, while tropical and subtropical regions have had a decrease of about 0.3% per decade. The number of heavy downpours (2 inches [5 cm] of rain in a single day) in the United States increased by 25% between 1900 and 2000.

As temperatures have risen, Northern Hemisphere snow cover has decreased by about 10% since the late 1960s and 1970s. The greatest decline is seen in spring: For example, 75% of sites in western North America have seen a reduction in springtime snowfall since 1950. Declining snow cover has also been found in Eurasia, including the Alps.

Ocean temperatures are rising at the surface and into the mid-depths. From 1955 to 1998, the upper 9,800 feet (3,000 m) of the ocean warmed by an average of about 0.067°F (0.037°C). While this may not seem like much, water's high heat capacity and the vastness of the seas mean that even a small temperature increase requires a large amount of heat. Climate models show that the oceans have absorbed 20 times as much heat as the atmosphere in the past 50 years.

CAUSES OF RECENT CLIMATE CHANGE

The rate of temperature increase is faster than it has been in at least one millennium and most likely faster than in two or more. When scientists construct climate models to reproduce the changes that are taking place, inputting only natural causes of climate change is not sufficient to replicate current conditions. Models that input only human-generated causes of climate change are also not sufficient. To reconstruct recent warming trends, models must take into account both natural climate variations and the rise in greenhouse gas levels due to human activities. Greenhouse gases have carried far more weight in determining modern climate than any other factor in the warming seen since 1950.

Due to increased fossil fuel and biomass burning, atmospheric CO_2 has been rising sharply since the Industrial Revolution. The total increase for that time period is 27%, from the preindustrial value of 280 ppm to the January 2007 value of 382 ppm. Nearly 65% of that rise has been since CO_2 was first measured on Mauna Loa volcano in Hawaii in 1958, when the value was 316 ppm. In fact, the rate of increase in CO_2 has doubled from 30 years ago. One of the largest single-year increases on record—a rise of 2.6 ppm—was in 2005.

The increase in atmospheric CO_2 measured above Mauna Loa since 1958 is known as the Keeling curve. The up-and-down annual cycle

A comparison between modeled and observed temperature rises between 1860 and 2000. The red line is the same in each graph; it is the observed temperature as measured by thermometers. In the first graph, the blue line shows the temperature that was modeled for that time period using only natural causes of warming. The temperature rise cannot be explained by natural causes alone. In the second graph, the blue line shows the temperature that was modeled for that time period using human activities (greenhouse gas emissions, primarily). The temperatures observed in the early- to mid-twentieth century cannot be explained by human activity alone. In the third graph, the blue line shows the temperature that was modeled for both natural causes and human activities. This is the best fit and shows that both categories of change are needed to model the temperature rise of the past 140 years.

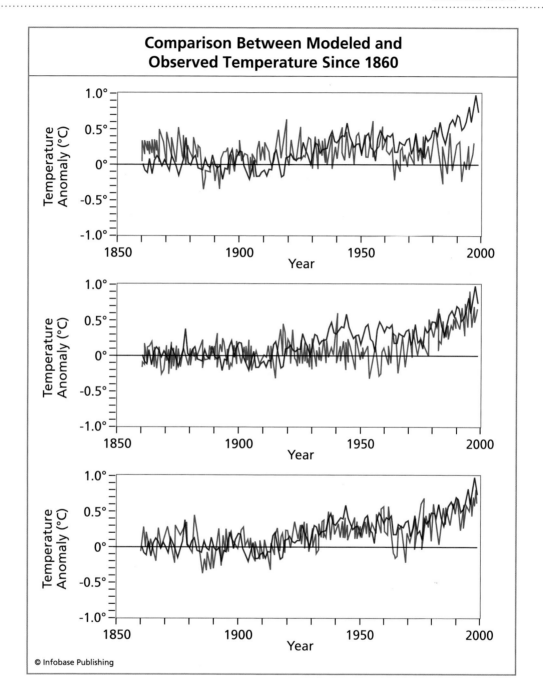

**Comparison Between Modeled and
Observed Temperature Since 1860**

© Infobase Publishing

is the result of the seasons. Most of the planet's land masses lie in the Northern Hemisphere. In spring, when the North Pole points toward the Sun, trees sprout leaves and grasses multiply. The growing plants absorb CO_2 from the atmosphere. In autumn, as the plants die back, the CO_2 is rereleased into the atmosphere. Like CO_2, methane amounts have risen since the Industrial Revolution; in this case, 151%, mostly from agricultural sources.

Scientists studying Greenland ice cores discovered in 2006 that there is more CO_2 in the atmosphere now than at any time in the past 650,000 years. During all that time, in fact, CO_2 had never risen

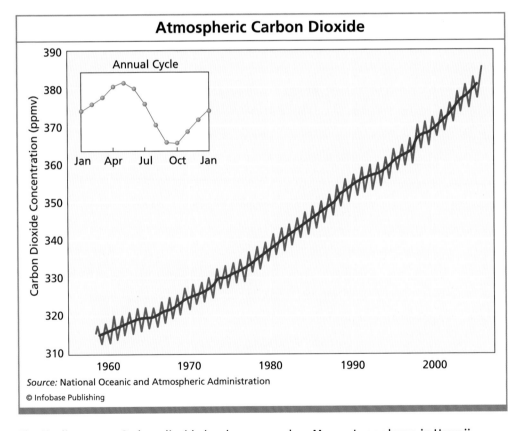

Source: National Oceanic and Atmospheric Administration

© Infobase Publishing

The Keeling curve. Carbon dioxide levels measured on Mauna Loa volcano in Hawaii increase steadily between 1958 and 2005. The annual cycle (shown in red) reflects the absorption of carbon in the spring and summer as plants grow, and the release of carbon in the fall and winter as they decay. The blue line represents the five-year mean value.

above 300 ppm. Analyses of Antarctic ice cores show that levels of the three most important greenhouse gases (CO_2, methane, and nitrous oxide) were never as high as they are today. It is important to note that greenhouse gases remain in the atmosphere for centuries.

When modeling recent climate change, scientists must take into account global dimming, which has the opposite effect on the climate from greenhouse warming. Global dimming causes a decrease in warming equal to about one-third the increase caused by greenhouse gases. The abundance of sulfate aerosols over the developed nations may explain why the Northern Hemisphere has warmed less than Southern Hemisphere; why the United States has experienced less warming than the rest of world; and why most global warming has occurred at night and not during the day, especially over polluted areas.

Of course, air pollution has harmful effects on the environment and human health. As a result, people in developed nations now regulate emissions so that the air above them and downwind is much less polluted. However, a decrease in air pollution also brings about a decrease in global dimming, and a decrease in global dimming is likely to increase global warming. Global dimming researchers think that recent improvements in the air quality of Western Europe may be responsible for recent temperature increases and even for the deadly European heat wave of the summer of 2003.

GREENHOUSE GAS LEVELS AND TEMPERATURE

As far back as scientists can measure CO_2 and temperature, it is clear that the two are related. A graph of CO_2 and temperature over the past 450,000 years (see the figure on page 52), shows just how close this correlation is. Although the relationship between the two is complicated, the result is clear. When CO_2 is high, temperatures are high; when CO_2 is low, temperatures are low.

A close look at the graph shows that, in the past, rising CO_2 has not usually triggered global warming. In fact, during interglacial periods, CO_2 begins to rise between 600 and 1,000 years after temperatures rise. Therefore, because a warming period takes about 5,000 years to complete, CO_2 may only be responsible for about 4,200 years of that warming. Other factors—a change in solar radiation intensity, Milankovitch cycles, or thermohaline circulation (which varies in different warming periods)—set off rising temperatures initially. Positive feedbacks then bring about a rise in CO_2 between 600 and 1,000 years later. These higher CO_2 levels cause temperatures to rise even higher. This leads to further positive feedbacks that result in the release of more CO_2 and still greater temperatures. Climate models support the idea that greenhouse gases cause about half of the warming that takes place between a glacial and an interglacial period.

Another question is raised by looking at the same figure: Why is CO_2 so much higher now than it has been in the past 450,000 years, and yet global temperatures have not climbed high enough to match CO_2 levels? The answer to this question is **thermal inertia**, which is the resistance a substance has to a change in temperature. Thermal inertia explains why even though the Northern Hemisphere receives the most sunlight on the summer solstice, the warmest summertime temperatures don't arrive until weeks later; or why, even though the Sun is directly overhead at noon, the hottest time of day comes several hours later. Simply put, greenhouse gas levels are rising so rapidly that the temperatures cannot keep up. The lag between increasing greenhouse gases and the rise of global temperatures appears to be a few decades. The thermal inertia in this case is primarily due to the high heat capacity of the oceans. The models show that global temperature will eventually catch up with greenhouse gas levels, and the full temperature response will be realized.

GREENHOUSE GAS EMISSIONS BY COUNTRY

Not all nations of the world are equally responsible for greenhouse gas emissions and global warming. The United States is the largest emitter of greenhouse gases, followed by the nations China and Russia. Researchers have been predicting that China will overtake the United States in CO_2 emissions by 2010. Some estimates suggest that this already took place in 2006.

Carbon Emissions by Nation, 2003

RANK	COUNTRY	CO_2 EMISSIONS (THOUSAND METRIC TONS)	PERCENTAGE OF WORLD TOTAL	PER CAPITA EMISSIONS (METRIC TONS)	RANK
	World Total	27,500,000			
1.	United States of America	5,819,272	21.2	19.8	11
2.	China	4,191,143	15.2	3.2	99
3.	Russia	1,495,870	5.4	10.3	31
4.	India	1,275,610	4.6	1.2	133
5.	Japan	1,233,640	4.5	9.7	36
6.	Germany	806,577	2.9	9.8	35
7.	Canada	566,617	2.1	17.9	13
8.	United Kingdom	559,524	2.0	9.4	38
9.	South Korea	456,751	1.7	9.6	37
10.	Italy	446,302	1.6	7.7	52
11.	Mexico	416,698	1.5	4.0	87
12.	Iran	382,092	1.4	5.6	69
13.	France	381,202	1.4	6.2	61
14.	South Africa	364,853	1.3	7.8	51
15.	Australia	354,731	1.3	18.0	12
16.	Ukraine	315,018	1.1	6.6	58
17.	Spain	309,751	1.1	7.3	54
18.	Poland	305,053	1.1	7.9	48
19.	Saudi Arabia	302,884	1.1	13.0	18
20.	Brazil	298,902	1.1	1.6	124

Source: United Nations Statistics Division

To calculate per capita emissions, a nation's total of CO_2 emissions is divided by the nation's population. The top 10 highest per capita emitters in the world are not even in the top 20 nations for total emissions. The reason is that they are small countries with high production and/or low energy efficiency. (Efficiency is the ratio of usable energy output to energy input.) Several of the top 10 per capita emitters are oil-rich nations—including Qatar, the United Arab Emirates, and Kuwait—that do not need to use petroleum efficiently. The nations with high total emissions but low per capita emissions, such as India, have very low productivity for the size of the nation's population.

The United States is an enormous emitter of CO_2, in part because it is the world's largest economy. But that does not tell the whole story, because the United States emits twice as much CO_2 to produce one unit of Gross National Product (GNP) as the nations of Western Europe. This means that the United States is only half as efficient in its energy use as Western Europe. Australia has low total emissions because it has such a low population, but it is nearly as inefficient with energy use as the United States.

WRAP-UP

Ice core data from the past 600,000 years show that when CO_2 is high, global temperatures are high. Although current CO_2 levels are higher than they have ever been, temperatures have not caught up with greenhouse gas levels due to thermal inertia. Scientists say that it is only a matter of time before temperatures rise to match atmospheric CO_2 levels. Even with thermal inertia, the hottest years of the last 1,000 years have been in the past two decades, and the numbers of temperature records that have recently been broken indicate that the trend is continuing. Nations vary greatly in the amount of greenhouse gas emissions that they add to the atmosphere, with the United States and China in the lead.

Without a doubt, the Earth's climate future will include the enormous impact that humans make on the atmosphere. Nearly all climate scientists agree that human influence will overshadow natural changes for at least a millennium, until Milankovitch and other natural cycles push the planet toward a new ice age.

PART TWO

VISIBLE EFFECTS
OF CLIMATE CHANGE

Effects of Climate Change on the Atmosphere and Hydrosphere

No single event can be attributed unequivocally to global warming: not ice melting, not an increase in hurricane intensity, not the bleaching of coral reefs. It is the sum of all of these changes collectively that points very strongly to a world in which global warming is having an increasing effect. The most dramatic impacts being felt so far in the atmosphere and hydrosphere are the melting cryosphere, rising seas, and the rise in extreme weather events.

Many of the observations presented in this chapter and the next were described in the Intergovernmental Panel on Climate Change (IPCC) Fourth Assessment. Much of what is presented in the report, and much of what is known about changes caused by warming temperature, comes from studies in the Northern Hemisphere because that is where the scientists are concentrated. Europeans, in particular, have been collecting information over decades and centuries that is useful today.

CRYOSPHERE

Warming at the poles has been much greater than warming in other parts of the globe, a phenomenon due largely to positive feedback mechanisms. The cryosphere is especially sensitive to warming temperature because of the water-ice transition. If the temperature in a tropical forest increases by a few degrees, the forest only becomes warmer. But where water is near its freezing point, a small temperature increase converts solid ice into liquid water. This, in turn, drastically reduces albedo, which further increases warming. Ice does not accumulate as easily on open water as it does on or near other ice. Each winter there is less ice, and the ice that forms is thinner, which makes increased melting likely when summer arrives.

Recent high latitude temperature increases have reduced ice and snow cover in the Arctic region. Satellite mapping of the extent of Arctic sea ice in September shows a 20% drop off since 1979, the first year satellite mapping was done, and an even greater decrease in

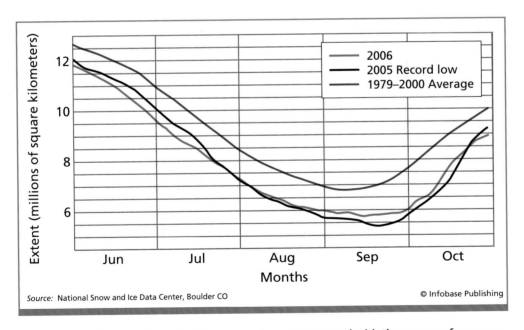

Source: National Snow and Ice Data Center, Boulder CO   © Infobase Publishing

Arctic summertime sea ice extent in 2005 and 2006 compared with the average from 1979 to 2000. The past several years have seen a large decrease in sea ice.

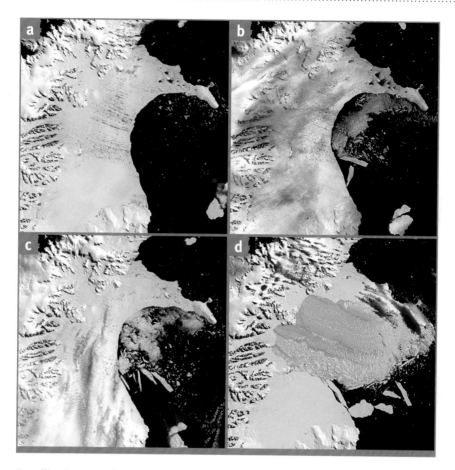

Satellite images show the breakup of the Larsen B ice shelf in 2002. The dates of the images are: a) January 31, b) February 17, c) February 23, and d) March 7. *(NASA)*

the past few years. Scientists report that their climate models cannot explain the great loss of sea ice without factoring in human-induced greenhouse gas emissions.

Antarctic sea ice has shown no consistent change in extent at this time. Yet, in parts of Antarctica, ice shelves are collapsing. The largest collapse since the end of the last glacial advance occurred off the Antarctic Peninsula in 2002. The Larsen B ice shelf was 1,255 square miles (3,250 sq. km), about the size of Rhode Island, and

650 feet (200 m) thick. Its collapse followed that of the Larsen A in 1995.

Glaciers and ice sheets have been in retreat at least since 1961. Beginning in 2000, the melting rate was 1.6 times more than the average rate of the 1990s, and three times the rate of the 1980s. Glaciers in the low latitudes are retreating most rapidly. Mount Kilimanjaro glacier, immortalized in Ernest Hemingway's short story "The Snows of Kilimanjaro," has capped the equatorial African mountain for the past 11,700 years. But this glacier has been retreating for at least a century, perhaps due to a decrease in atmospheric moisture over that part of Africa. More recently, melting due to global warming has added to and speeded up the process. In all, the ice cap shrank from 4.71 square miles (12.1 sq. km) in 1912 to 0.68 square miles (1.76 sq. km) in 2006. Ohio State University's Lonnie Thompson has witnessed the acceleration of the rate of ice loss and predicts the end of the snows of Kilimanjaro at around 2015. At that time, all that remains of Kilimanjaro's glaciers will be in an Ohio State University freezer.

Snowfall has increased in the interior of Greenland and portions of Antarctica, yet ice sheets in both locations are shrinking back. Warmer temperatures melt the ice sheets at their edges, while melt water traveling between the ice sheet and the underlying rock causes the ice to slip at its base and enter the melting zone more rapidly. Between 2003 and 2005, Greenland's low coastal areas lost about three times more weight in ice than the interior accumulated as snow. The net annual ice melt is equal to the volume of water that flows through the Colorado River in 12 years.

Northern Hemisphere permafrost is thawing, turning portions of the Arctic that were frozen for thousands of years into **wetlands**. (Wetlands are poorly drained landscapes that

Karango camp of Mt. Kilimanjaro. (*Dreamstime.com*)

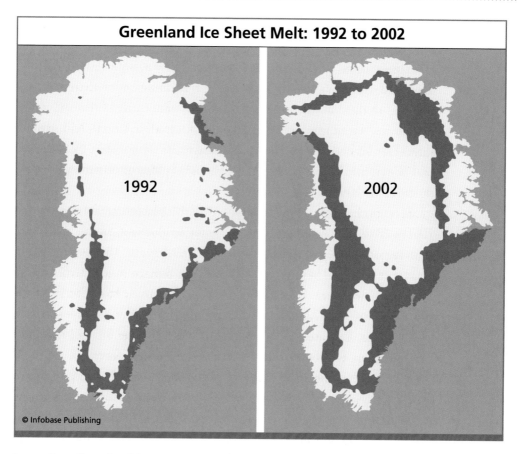

Ice melt on Greenland in 2002 was much more extensive than ice melt in 1992.

are covered all or a large portion of the year with fresh or salt water.) There is evidence that the southern extent of permafrost in the Yukon of Canada has moved poleward a distance of 60 miles (100 km) since 1899, although accurate records go back only 30 years. The loss of permafrost intensifies Arctic runoff and **erosion** because frozen lands are more stable. (Erosion is the transport of sediments from their original location by wind, precipitation, ice, or gravity.) Melting permafrost is a positive feedback mechanism for global warming because it releases methane and other hydrocarbon greenhouse gases into the atmosphere.

WATER CYCLE AND WATER RESOURCES

Less water trapped in ice means that more water winds up in the other reservoirs, such as the atmosphere, streams and lakes, and the oceans. Generally, the water cycle is becoming more extreme: Wet regions are becoming wetter, and dry regions are becoming drier. Europe is wetter and is experiencing increased runoff and stream flow. The United States has weathered a 20% increase in blizzards and heavy rainstorms since 1900; the total amount of winter precipitation is up 10%.

By contrast, dry areas have more than doubled in size since the 1970s. Arid and semiarid regions, such as Africa's Sahel, are experiencing increased drought. Reduced rainfall in the southwestern United States has lowered Colorado River flow to less than it was in the Dust Bowl years of the mid-1930s. For five millennia, the Hamoun wetlands, covering 1,500 square miles (4,000 sq. km) and containing ample water, fish, and game, were a place of refuge for the people of Central Asia. The removal of water for irrigation before it could enter the wetlands, coupled with intense droughts, turned the area into a region of salt flats in 2002.

Warmer air has increased the temperature of surface water in the Northern Hemisphere's lakes and rivers by about 0.3 to 3.6°F (0.2 to 2°C) since the 1960s. The ice on large lakes and rivers in the mid and high latitudes now freezes nine days later, breaks up 10 days earlier, and is thinner and less extensive than in the past. In some East African lakes, deep water has also warmed, which can affect deep aquatic life. This trend will likely be seen in other lakes.

Warmer temperatures change the thermal structure of lakes. A warm surface layer is not dense enough to sink, so its ability to mix with the colder deeper layers is reduced. This keeps oxygen out of the deep layers of the lake and causes aquatic life to suffer. Water quality also decreases in the lake surface (where most organisms live) as solids, salts, and pollutants collect and are no longer mixed throughout the lake.

Rivers are also experiencing changes due to rising temperatures. Due to shorter winters, snow melts earlier in spring, and river flow peaks earlier in the year. Because communities typically need more water in summer, when there is less rainfall, this shift puts a strain on water supply systems.

Water systems will soon be strained by shrinking glaciers. The people of the Andes Mountains of South America rely on snow and ice melt for their water during the dry summers. Runoff is currently high because the glaciers are melting back at about 328 feet (100 m) per decade. By the end of this decade, however, some glaciers will be gone or too small to provide much meltwater. Himalayan glaciers are also melting. These glaciers feed seven rivers that provide more than half the drinking water for 40% of the world's people.

OCEANS

Warmer air has raised temperatures in the upper levels of the oceans 0.9°F (0.5°C) over the past four to five decades and increased global SST an average of 0.18°F to 0.36°F (0.1°C to 0.2°C) since 1976. Although the variability of SST is natural, the rise since the 1970s cannot be explained by natural causes. Warming ocean temperatures have resulted in rising sea level, increased erosion, and a change in deep ocean circulation.

Warmer temperatures instigate sea level rise for two reasons: melting ice and **thermal expansion**. Melting ice from glaciers and ice sheets adds extra water to the oceans, although meltwater from ice shelves and sea ice, which float atop the sea, does not. Thermal expansion is a change in the volume of water. Like all substances, water molecules vibrate more vigorously as their temperature increases. The molecules take up more space, causing the water to swell. Although this effect is small, on an oceanwide scale, thermal expansion can swell the sea significantly and result in a sea level rise. Due to thermal expansion and melting glaciers, sea level has risen about eight inches (20 cm) in the past century, and the rate of upsurge has increased in recent years. In June 2006, scientists announced that the sea level rose, on average, 0.1 inches (0.3 cm) per year between 1993 and 2005. Scientists say that natural variations, such as changing wind patterns

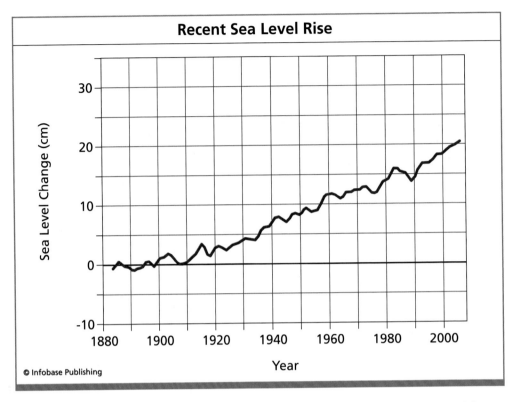

Recent Sea Level Rise

Sea Level Change (cm)

30

20

10

0

-10

1880   1900   1920   1940   1960   1980   2000

Year

© Infobase Publishing

Recent sea level rise. The rise in sea level in centimeters from 1880 to 2005. The red line represents the three-year average.

and El Niño–Southern Oscillation (ENSO) events, account for only a small part of this increase.

Higher sea level poses a problem during storms because waves and **storm surge** take place at a level relatively higher to the land. (Storm surge is a local rise in sea level due to winds blowing water up against a shoreline.) Higher storm surge and waves cause flooding, erosion, and the loss of wetlands. Rising seas caused by climate change could destroy half the **mangrove** forests on some Pacific islands; although, so far, the changing of mangrove forests into shrimp farms has had a far greater effect on tropical coastlines. In the past two decades, 35% of the world's mangrove forests have been lost.

Globally, 70% of the world's sandy beaches are eroding. Sea level rise is partly to blame, but other human activities bring greater damage. These include the loss of natural features that protect the shoreline, such as mangrove forests and coral reefs; sediment starvation due to dam construction on rivers; and subsidence due to groundwater pumping. Beach loss is bad for coastal communities, and protecting shorelines has become a major enterprise in the countries that can afford it.

EXTREME WEATHER

Warmer temperatures have increased extreme weather events in their frequency, severity, and longevity. Warmer air holds more water and circulates more vigorously than cooler air, both of which factors are conducive to creating storms. There is evidence that the past few decades have seen an increase in extreme weather. For example, insurance companies now pay 15 times more money to the victims of extreme weather than they did three decades ago. The total economic losses, including those that are noninsured, are also far greater. One major reason for the enormous increase in economic losses is that there is much more development to which losses can occur, particularly near coastlines.

Heat Waves

The deadliest weather phenomena are heat waves, which have increased in frequency and duration in recent years. A heat wave is a prolonged period of excessively hot weather, relative to what is expected for that location. In temperate zones, a heat wave is considered to be at least three consecutive days of 86°F (30°C) weather, but in warmer regions much hotter temperatures are required.

Despite the prevalence of heating and air conditioning to moderate indoor climate in the developed world, temperature extremes still sometimes lead to lethal results. Health is most impacted when nighttime temperatures remain high, and the heat does not subside for days.

Famous for its sunshine, Athens, Greece, was struck by an unusual winter snowstorm in January 2006. Famous tourist sites, such as the Acropolis and its Parthenon temple, were shut down by the storm. *(Aris Messinis/AFP/Getty Images)*

The increase in pollutants in the stagnant air further contributes to the problem of high temperatures. High heat is also more damaging when coupled with high humidity. The summer of 2003 in Europe was the hottest since 1500. Estimates are that around 26,000 people—nearly 15,000 in France alone—died of heat-related problems. The total cost of the disaster was estimated at $13.5 billion.

Drought

A region is considered to be in a drought if it has had a shortage of rainfall for days, weeks, seasons, or years when compared with how much rain usually falls. Drought is also related to the effectiveness of the rain. For example, if a drought-stricken region receives its entire annual rainfall in one quick storm, the water runs off the land before it can soak into the soil and provide moisture for plants, and the area remains in drought. The National Center for Atmospheric Research in Boulder, Colorado, reports that about 30% of the world's lands are now stricken by drought, double from the percentage in the 1970s. The southwestern United States has been experiencing drought conditions since 1998.

Floods

While warming has parched some regions, others have experienced increased flooding. There were 10 times as many catastrophic floods between 1990 and 2000 globally than in an average decade between 1950 and 1985. The number of people affected by floods worldwide has risen to 150 million from 7 million in the 1960s. The increase has mostly taken place on the world's largest rivers.

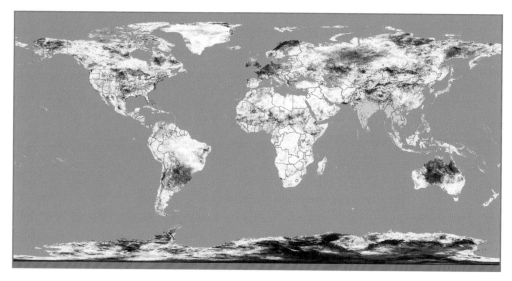

This map from NASA shows temperature anomalies from July 12–19, 2006, when compared with averages from those dates from the six summers from 2000 to 2005 in the midwestern United States, western Europe, and across eastern Siberia. Air temperatures in the midwestern United States soared past 100°F (40°C); Britain, Germany, and the Netherlands experienced their hottest July on record; and Australia was devastated by the prevailing hot, dry conditions. *(NASA / Jesse Allen, Earth Observatory, using data provided courtesy of Zhengming Wan, MODIS Land Surface Temperature Group, Institute of Computational Earth System Science, University of California, Santa Barbara)*

Flooding of the Mississippi River in Gurnee, Illinois, in 2004. (© *Gary Braasch, from the* book *Earth Under Fire: How Global Warming Is Changing the World*, *University of California Press, 2007*)

The 1993 Mississippi River flood was the most damaging in United States history due to recent development along the river. The river basin received between two and six times the normal amount of rainfall—so much rain that the ground became too saturated to absorb more water, and local streams began to overflow. As many as 150 levees, protecting over 6,000 miles (9,300 km) of the Mississippi and its tributaries, failed. However, not all levees broke, and low-lying areas in Davenport, Iowa; Rock Island, Illinois; and Hannibal, Missouri, among others, were saved. At least some of the extreme flooding was caused by the 80% loss of Mississippi River basin wetlands, which once acted as natural floodwater storage.

Hurricanes

The costliest and most visible change in weather-related disasters in the United States is the increase in the number of intense hurricanes making landfall from the Atlantic basin. Similar increases are also occurring in the Pacific basin.

Hurricanes are born in summer and autumn when a vast area of the sea surface rises to 82°F (28°C) or higher, and winds are light. The warm seawater heats the air above it, causing the air to rise. The column of air spirals upward, feeding on the heat energy from the tropical waters. For the storm to grow, there must be little or no wind shear between the lower and upper atmosphere; high wind shear will decapitate the storm.

Hurricanes can grow to 350 miles (600 km) in diameter and 50,000 feet (15 km) in height. Hurricanes are categorized on the Saffir-Simpson scale, which is presented in the table on page 87. Wind speed is highly significant because a storm with 130-miles-per-hour

(209 kph) winds has almost double the strength of one with 100-miles-per-hour (160 kph) winds. As a result, although they are only 20% of the storms that make landfall, Category 4 and 5 storms produce more than 80% of the damage from hurricanes. Rainfall of one inch (2.5 cm) per hour is not uncommon in a large storm, and a single hurricane may produce a deluge of up to 22 billion tons (20 billion metric tons) of

The Saffir-Simpson Hurricane Scale

CATEGORY	MAXIMUM SUSTAINED WIND SPEED		DAMAGE
	(MPH)	(KPH)	
1 (weak)	74–95	119–153	Above normal; no real damage to structures
2 (moderate)	96–110	154–177	Some roofing, door, and window damage; considerable damage to vegetation, mobile homes, and piers
3 (strong)	111–130	178–209	Some buildings damaged; mobile homes destroyed
4 (very strong)	131–156	210–251	Complete roof failure on small residences; major erosion of beach areas; major damage to lower floors of structures
5 (devastating)	>156	>251	Complete roof failure on many residences and industrial buildings; some complete building failures

Source: National Oceanic and Atmospheric Administration (NOAA)

water a day. Hurricanes typically last 5 to 10 days but may last up to three weeks. Once these mighty storms are cut off from warm water, they lose strength, so they die fairly quickly over cooler water or land.

Damage comes from the impact of these storms on the ocean as well. Category 4 and 5 hurricanes can generate storm surges of 20 to 25 feet (7.0 to 7.6 m) for a distance of 50 to 100 miles (80 to 160 km) along a coastline. Giant waves, up to 50 feet (15 m) high, ride atop storm surges and cause even greater damage. In areas of low elevation—as is typical of the Atlantic and Gulf Coasts of the United States, which rise less than 10 feet (3 m) above sea level—flooding may be devastating.

A typical Atlantic season spawns six hurricanes and many smaller tropical storms. On average, one hurricane strikes the United States coastline three times in every five years (that is, there is a 60% chance of a hurricane striking the coastline in any given year). But few hurricane seasons are typical. A cycle of high activity from the 1920s through the 1960s was followed by low activity between 1971 and 1994. Nevertheless, major storms can form during quiet periods, as was shown when Hurricane Andrew devastated South Florida in 1992.

Since 1995, conditions have become much more favorable for hurricane growth. Between 1995 and 2000, hurricanes formed at a rate twice as great as during the most recent quiet period, and the Caribbean experienced a fivefold increase. Some hurricane experts attribute variations in storm number to natural climate variation, such as the Atlantic Multidecadal Oscillation (AMO), rather than to global warming.

Still, many experts blame global warming for other changes in hurricanes. A 2005 study in the journal *Nature,* by Kerry Emanuel of the Massachusetts Institute of Technology, shows that hurricanes have increased in duration and intensity by about 50% since the 1970s. The number of Category 4 and 5 hurricanes jumped from 50 per five years during the 1970s to 90 per five years since 1995. The jump was even higher in the North Atlantic, from 16 strong hurricanes between 1975 and 1989 to 26 between 1990 and 2004.

Emanuel's study and others have shown that hurricane number may be related to some other climate oscillation, but that hurricane intensity is related to global warming. Seasons with high SST and global air

Sea surface temperature view, showing Hurricane Katrina as it moves over Gulf of Mexico waters on its way to the Louisiana and Mississippi coasts, August 27, 2005. Color indicates water temperature, with deep oranges as the hottest temperatures and deep blues as the coldest. *(NASA/Goddard Space Flight Center Scientific Visualization Studio)*

temperature have intense storms. Rising temperatures also cause these mammoth storms to last longer. These effects of increased storm intensity and duration are predicted by computer models of rising SST.

In the hurricane season of 2005, SST in the critical portions of the Atlantic basin were 1.6°F (0.9°C) higher than was the average between 1901 and 1970. Not surprisingly, perhaps, the 2005 hurricane season has become known as the longest and most damaging season ever (through 2006). The 2005 season lasted weeks past the normal end of hurricane season. There were so many storms that, for the first time, the World Meteorological Organization ran out of the 21 previously chosen names that are available each hurricane season, with the result that six storms needed to be identified by letters of the Greek alphabet. Seven major hurricanes made landfall, resulting in nearly 2,300 deaths and damages of more than $100 billion. Hurricane Wilma was the most intense storm ever recorded, and the third costliest. The costliest, Hurricane Katrina, was the most damaging natural disaster to strike the United States to date. (But not the deadliest: The hurricane that hit Galveston, Texas, in 1900 is estimated to have killed more than 6,000 people. That high death toll was due, in part, to the fact that it took place long before meteorologists were able to predict hurricanes.)

A study by Kevin Trenberth and Dennis Shea of the National Center for Atmospheric Research, in Boulder, Colorado, published in *Geophysical Research Letters* in 2006, analyzed the reasons the 2005 season was so unusual. It suggests that global warming played the biggest role, with a smaller effect from a Pacific El Niño and a still smaller effect from the AMO. Climate scientists will likely be debating the relative impacts of global warming and other factors regarding hurricanes for years to come.

The United States is not the only location experiencing unusual hurricane activity. In 2004, Japan experienced 10 typhoons, three more than the greatest number ever recorded. Also that year, for the first time, a hurricane formed in the South Atlantic. That storm, called Hurricane Catarina, hit Brazil.

WRAP-UP

Earth is always changing, on both long and short timescales. Glaciers grow and melt, sea level rises and falls, and hurricanes come and go. But the adjectives are starting to line up: The hottest, driest, wettest, and stormiest weather in history is being experienced in many different locales. These phenomena are pointing in one direction; the effects of global warming are becoming apparent and more intense in the atmosphere and the hydrosphere. And such changes are beginning to take a toll on the biosphere, as will be discussed in the following chapter.

Effects of
Climate Change
on the Biosphere

Scientists working in the field of climate change response say that they are already seeing the effects of climate change on living systems. These effects are documented on every continent, in every ocean, across ecosystems, and in every major group of organisms. This chapter discusses the impacts of warming climate on the biosphere—impacts that match the predictions made by climate change models. Scientists see the effects of climate change on individual organisms, on species of organisms, and on entire ecosystems. Although temperature increases thus far have been small, a large percentage of the species studied have shown some response to climate change.

EFFECTS ON ORGANISMS

Organisms are adapted to live in particular environmental conditions. Polar bears (*Ursus maritimus*) need to walk across sea ice to hunt; and corals need water that is warm, with just the right salinity. When conditions change, organisms need to change, or they may die out locally or even go extinct. Scientists who study the effects of global warming on the biosphere have discovered that the processes of evolution do not work fast enough for organisms to adapt to rapidly changing climate. At most, species may evolve a greater ability to disperse into new geographic locations. For example, two species of bush crickets in the United Kingdom evolved longer wings in their northern range boundary. The longer wings allowed the crickets to travel to new territory farther north.

The most common response, then, that a species has to warmer temperatures is to move to a cooler location, either higher latitudes or higher elevations. The fossil record indicates that changing latitude or altitude was a common response of organisms to climate change in the past. Of course, this strategy does not always work because the environment in the direction the organisms move may turn out to be unsuitable. Land-based species could find their way to favorable conditions blocked by an impassable ocean or extended out of reach beyond the top of a mountain. The situation is now more complicated than it was in prior Earth history because people have altered the environment with farms, ranches, and cities that may be incompatible with the species' needs.

A species also may respond to climate change by altering the timing of phases of its life cycle, so that it breeds earlier in the spring, for example. This does not necessarily help it better adapt to the new circumstances; it only reflects the way the species is evolutionarily programmed to respond to weather cues: to breed when the nighttime low temperature rises above freezing for several days in a row, for example. The science of how climate influences the recurrence of annual events in the life cycles of plants and animals is called **phenology**. Some of the findings of phenology as they concern global warming are discussed below.

Freshwater Organisms

Increased temperatures have brought conflicting changes to the aquatic life in some lakes. For example, with a longer growing season and less ice cover, a lake may have more algal growth and therefore higher primary productivity. (**Algae** are a very diverse group of organisms they are not plants, but most algae photosynthesize.) However, the warm water may remain at the surface, so that there is less mixing of nutrients, which may cause a decrease in productivity.

Warming temperatures have changed the phenology of some freshwater species. In large lakes, the phytoplankton population explodes in the spring, after mixing brings nutrients from deep water to the surface, and when the springtime sunlight becomes strong enough to support photosynthesis. To take advantage of the abundant food, zooplankton populations mushroom just after the spring phytoplankton bloom begins. Now, with spring arriving earlier than in the past, the phytoplankton bloom occurs up to four weeks earlier, but the zooplankton bloom has not kept up. By the time the zooplankton emerge, the phytoplankton populations have already peaked, and the zooplankton starve. Because zooplankton are food for the small fish that serve as food for larger fish, a loss of zooplankton can cause a collapse of the local food web. However, in some lakes, zooplankton populations have increased, and fish populations have grown. Some species of fish, both wild and farmed, have also changed their spring life cycle patterns.

Warming temperatures in rivers have affected the abundance, distribution, and migration patterns of some fish species. In some rivers, warm water species are replacing cold water species. Migrations may take place up to six weeks earlier in some fish populations. Populations that experience such a large change in timing typically suffer higher mortality rates in fish and their spawn.

Marine Organisms

In marine organisms, variations in abundance, productivity, and phenology are strongly influenced by short-term climatic variations, such as the El Niño-Southern Oscillation (ENSO) and the North Atlantic Oscillation (NAO). Separating these influences from those due to greenhouse warming is sometimes difficult. Nevertheless, scientists say that several effects are largely due to global warming. NASA estimates that global plankton productivity has decreased at least 6% to 9% in the past 25 years due to rising SST. Warmer temperatures are also causing marine plankton and fish to move toward the poles. One large, recent study found that North Atlantic species moved northward by 10° latitude in 40 years. While overfishing is the cause of the collapse of the once copious North Atlantic cod (*Gadus* sp.) population, warming temperatures may be working against the species' recovery. Recent declines in plankton numbers may be a factor in the poor survival rates of cod larvae.

The warming of the air over the Antarctic Peninsula by 4.5°F (2.5°C) in the past 50 years has greatly affected life in the Southern Ocean. **Krill** (*Euphausia superba*), an extremely abundant type of zooplankton, form the base of the Southern Ocean food web and are the favorite food of some whales. Since 1976, warming temperatures have reduced the extent of sea ice, which has reduced the habitat required for the ice algae that are a favorite food of the krill. This has been one factor in the 80% decline of krill in the southwestern Atlantic, where they have been historically concentrated. The decrease in krill numbers has opened up the seas for an increase in salps. These jellylike organisms are not a good source of food for fish and other organisms higher up the food web. As a result, populations of seabirds and seals are in decline.

Many marine plankton species have advanced the timing of their seasonal behavior. Just as in large lakes, when the zooplankton no longer emerge in time to take advantage of the phytoplankton bloom, the zooplankton population suffers. The loss of zooplankton for the food web has negatively affected populations of fish, seabirds, and marine mammals. The migrations of some species of marine animals are also changing; migrations have been found to occur one to two months earlier in warm years.

Nearshore organisms are also showing the effects of warming. In the Pacific, the species found in the intertidal, kelp forest, and offshore zooplankton communities are shifting their ranges due to warmer temperatures. Sea anemones, for example, are moving into California's Monterey Bay, where the water was previously too cool. The richest ecosystems in the oceans, coral reefs, are being damaged by rising ocean temperatures.

Global Warming Dead Zone

Scientists at Oregon State University are blaming warming temperatures for a **dead zone** that has formed in coastal waters off the state. As of 2006, the dead zone was 1,234 square miles (1985 sq. km), about the size of Rhode Island. In that year, it made its first appearance in the coastal region of Washington State. The dead zone recurred in 2007 but was not as large or intense as the 2006 event.

A survey by scientists using a remotely operated underwater vehicle found rotting Dungeness crabs (*Cancer magister*) and sea worms, and a complete lack of fish in the area. "Thousands and thousands of dead crabs and molts were littering the ocean floor, many sea stars were dead, and the fish have either left the area or have died and been washed away," Professor Jane Lubchenko, who was involved in the study, said in a 2006 press release from Oregon State University.

Oceanic dead zones are caused by extremely low levels of oxygen in a region's waters. Without oxygen, most marine organisms suffocate. The Oregon dead zone is different from most dead zones, including the much larger one in the Gulf of Mexico. In the gulf, Mississippi River waters carry loads of excess nutrients from fertilizers, detergents, and runoff from feedlots into the water, causing an algae bloom. When these algae die, they are decomposed by bacteria and other organisms that use up all the water's oxygen.

In the Oregon dead zone, warmer air has changed ocean circulation. In normal years, southerly winds push surface water toward the shore, which keeps deep, nutrient-rich, oxygen-poor waters down below. These southerly winds alternate with northerly winds that then push the surface water out to sea. This brings the nutrient-rich, oxygen-poor water to the surface and allows it to mix with the normal surface nutrient-poor, oxygen-rich waters, providing an ideal environment for phytoplankton to bloom (but not overbloom) and support a healthy food web and marine fishery. In dead zone years, all the winds come from the north, and the nutrient-rich, oxygen-poor waters rise to the surface. Plankton bloom and feed off the nutrients, but when they die, they are decomposed by bacteria that take in the oxygen that remains in the water. As a result, oxygen levels dip as low as 10 to 30 times below normal: In one location, they were near zero.

Although they are far from certain, scientists say that changes in the jet stream due to global warming is the likeliest explanation.

Terrestrial Organisms

Warmer temperatures have increased growing seasons, with spring arriving earlier and fall coming later for many species of land plants and animals. The second half of the twentieth century saw an increase in growing season of up to two weeks in the mid and high latitudes, with many more frost-free days. The length of a growing season at a single research station in Spain increased by 32 days between 1952 and 2000, and the average increase across Europe was from 1.1 to

Coral Reefs

Coral reefs are known as the "rain forests of the sea" because they harbor such an incredible abundance and diversity of life. These spectacular and beautiful ecosystems are home to more than one-fourth of all marine plant and animal species. Reefs are built of tiny coral animals called **polyps** that construct calcium carbonate ($CaCO_3$) shells around their bodies. When the larva from a young coral polyp attaches itself to a good spot, usually on an existing coral, and builds a shell, the reef grows. The coral polyps enjoy a mutually beneficial relationship with minute algae called **zooxanthellae**. In this relationship, the photosynthetic algae supply oxygen and food to the corals, and the corals provide a home and nutrients (their wastes) for the zooxanthellae. The algae give the coral their bright colors of pink, yellow, blue, purple, and green. Coral polyps sometimes feed by capturing and eating the plankton that drift into their tentacles.

Corals can thrive only in a narrow set of conditions. They are very temperature sensitive, so the water must be warm, but not too hot. Water depth must be fairly shallow, with moderately high but constant salinity. The zooxanthellae must have clear, well-lit water to photosynthesize. Coral reefs protect shorelines from erosion and provide breeding, feeding, and nursery areas for commercially valuable fish and shellfish.

Damaged coral reefs sometimes turn white, a phenomenon called **coral bleaching**. First recognized in 1983, coral bleaching has become quite common. When coral animals are stressed, they expel their zooxanthellae. Since these algae give the coral its color, only the white limestone is left when they are gone. Sometimes zooxanthellae move back in when conditions improve, but if they are gone for too long, the corals starve and the reef dies. Coral reefs may recover from

4.9 days per decade. Longer growing seasons and warmer temperatures are sometimes accompanied by higher productivity, range changes, and earlier spring and summer seasonal events.

The total effect of growing season length on productivity is unclear. Satellite data show that a lengthened growing season caused increased productivity in the Northern Hemisphere from 1982 to 1991. However, from 1991 to 2002, productivity decreased there, possibly due to hotter, drier summers and more widespread droughts.

one bleaching event, but multiple events can kill them. Disease in corals and some other reef organisms has increased, especially in reefs that are already stressed.

Dr. Clive Wilkinson, coordinator of the Global Coral Reef Monitoring Network, blames the current upsurge in coral bleaching on rising seawater temperatures due to global warming. An increase in summer maximum temperatures of 1.8°F (1°C) for two to three days can trigger a coral bleaching event. If the elevated temperatures persist for less than one month, the reef will likely recover, but sustained heat will cause irreversible damage. After some high-temperature episodes, the resident zooxanthellae have been replaced by a more heat-tolerant species, and so the reef survives. However, many reefs are already found in the warmest water that zooxanthellae can tolerate, so this process is unlikely to save many reefs in the long run.

Bleaching of the Great Barrier Reef, Australia, in 2005. (© *Gary Braasch, from the book* Earth Under Fire: How Global Warming Is Changing the World, *University of California Press, 2007*)

According to Wilkinson's report, *Status of Coral Reefs of the World: 2004*, 20% of coral reefs are severely damaged and unlikely to recover, and another 24% are at imminent risk of collapse.

A wide variety of plants and animals have undergone recent range changes due to rising temperatures. An analysis of more than 1,700 species by Camille Parmesan of the University of Texas, Austin, and Gary Yohe of the University of Middletown, Connecticut, published in *Nature* in 2003, concluded that there has been a northward range shift of 3.8 miles (6.1 km) per decade. In tundra communities, a shift toward the poles or up mountains may result in a small decrease in range or replacement by trees and small shrubs. North American animals with ranges that are shifting northward include pikas (*Ochotona* sp.), Rufous hummingbirds (*Selasphorus rufus*), sea stars (of the class Asteroidea), and red foxes (*Vulpes vulpes*). Species of plants and animals that have never before been seen in the Arctic are moving in, such as mosquitoes and the American robin (*Turdus migratorius*). Antarctic plants have increased in abundance and range in the past few decades.

Species are disappearing in the lower latitude portions of their ranges. In North America, the Edith's checkerspot butterfly (*Euphydryas editha*) is almost extinct in Mexico but thriving in Canada. Adélie penguins are now thriving at their southernmost locations but have experienced large population declines where they are found farthest north on the Antarctic Peninsula.

Organisms are also moving up in altitude. Besides contracting in the southern end of their range, many more populations of Edith's checkerspot butterfly are becoming extinct in the lower elevation portions of their range (40%) than in the highest portions of their range (less than 15%). As a result, the mean elevation of the butterfly has moved upwards by 344 feet (105 m). In the Great Basin of the United States, the lower elevation populations of pika (*Ochotona princeps*) that were documented in the 1930s were extinct by the early 2000s because the animals have been found to die when the temperature reaches 88°F (31°C) for more than one-half hour. In the Alps, native plant species have been driven off mountaintops as they search for favorable conditions and as nonnative plant species move uphill.

Migrating animals are changing their ranges. Increasing numbers of European blackcap warblers (*Syliva atricapilla*) that have traditionally

The Apollo butterfly (*Parnassius apollo*) is changing its range within Europe. *(Bachmeier / Taxi / Getty Images)*

wintered in Africa are now migrating west to Great Britain. Chiff-chaffs (*Phylloscopus collybita*) no longer migrate south, but remain in the United Kingdom for the winter. Of the 57 species of European butterflies Parmesan studied, the ranges of 35 of them were migrating northward: For example, the Apollo (*Parnassius apollo*), moved 125 miles in 20 years. The Purple Emperor (*Apatura iris*), unknown in Sweden until the early 1990s, has been increasing its population there. African species, such as the Plain Tiger (*Danaus chrysippus*), have moved into Spain.

In some species, life cycle events that are tied to day length or temperature are now occurring at different times. The springtime emergence of insects, egg laying in birds, and mating in all animal types are events that have advanced to earlier in the spring. Parmesan and

Yoye detected an advancement of spring events of 2.3 days per decade averaged for all species and 5.1 days per decade averaged only for species that showed a change. These changes have been seen in plants, such as lupines (*Lupinus* sp.); insects, such as crickets and aphids; amphibians; and birds. For example, frogs in eastern North America and in England have been found to breed weeks earlier than they did early in the twentieth century. In mammals, high latitude and altitude species show the most changes. For example, yellow-bellied marmots (*Marmota flaviventris*) in the Rocky Mountains emerged from their winter hibernation 23 days earlier from 1975 to 1999.

Phenology is relatively easy to study in birds because the animals are visible, and their life cycles are highly regulated by seasonal changes. In many species, temperatures and conditions on the wintering grounds determine spring migration dates. British observers have noted that migratory birds now arrive in their breeding grounds 2 to 3 weeks earlier than they did 30 years ago. The egg-laying dates of these birds have also advanced—an average of 8.8 days for 20 species between 1971 and 1995.

In some European flycatchers, the egg-laying dates match trends in local temperature. For each 3.6°F (2°C) rise in temperature, the birds lay their eggs two days earlier. Unfortunately, the life cycles of the plants and invertebrates that these birds rely on for food have advanced even more, by about six days for each 3.6°F (2°C) rise in temperature. This timing discrepancy may, at some point, cause problems for the birds because their young will hatch well after their food sources peak. Already in some species, such as pied flycatchers (*Ficedula hypoleuca*), the number of young birds that hatch each year is smaller.

In some vulnerable locations, changing temperatures have led to the loss of suitable **habitats**, which is having a dramatic impact on some species. (A habitat is the natural environment of an organism, including the climate, resource availability, feeding interactions, and other features.) The loss of arctic sea ice, for example, is destroying the habitat that is needed by polar bears and northern seals. In the southern edge of their range, where ice is melting and hunting time is reduced, polar bear populations are in significant declines, and their mean body weight is decreasing. In addition, warmer temperatures have caused the populations of ringed seals, the bears' main food, to decline. In the northern portions of their range, significant numbers of polar bears have drowned because they are unable to swim the greater distances between ice floes. These more northerly polar bears are also experiencing lower reproductive success and lower body weight.

The direct effects of temperature changes affect animals differently. Populations of some birds increase when temperatures are high. But, as scientists have learned from El Niño events, when eastern Pacific Ocean temperatures are high, whales have less reproductive success. Some species experience mixed effects: Emperor penguins have greater hatching success when water temperatures rise, but the

Phenological Changes Seen in Some Species in Some Locations

CHANGE	TIMING
Average spring phenology	2.5 days advance per 1.8°F (1°C)
Spring phenology	2.3 or 5.1 days per decade
Leaf unfolding/flowers blooming	78% advanced, 22% delayed
Fruit ripening	75% advanced, 25% delayed
Leaf coloring (autumn arrival)	1 day later per 1.8°F (1°C)
Lengthening of growing season	1.1 to 4.9 days per decade (since 1951)
Leaf unfolding and flowering	1 to 3 days per decade
Bird species spring migration	1.3 to 4.4 days per decade
Bird species breeding	1.9 to 4.8 days per decade
Egg-laying dates	4 days per decade (1971 to 1995)

Source: Camille Parmesan. *"Ecological and Evolutionary Responses to Recent Climate Change,"* Annual Review of Ecological and Evolutionary Systems, *2006.*

birds must swim farther from shore to feed, which puts a great strain on them. Also, the instability of ice shelves has reduced nesting success. These competing forces have resulted in a 70% decrease in emperor penguin populations since the 1960s.

AGRICULTURE

Agricultural technology has increased so much in the past few decades that any changes that have resulted from rising temperatures and CO_2 levels are not easily discernable. Small adjustments that farmers make due to temperature increases have likely been absorbed by all the other changes. Yet some recent adaptations to warmer temperatures have been seen in agriculture.

The number of frost-free nights has increased in the temperate regions, resulting in a one week longer growing season in parts of North America relative to a few decades ago. Crop yields in the temperate regions, where developed nations are largely located, have increased. In Europe, particularly at high latitudes, farmers have adapted to environmental changes by planting their crops earlier. In Germany, for example, the advance has been 2.1 days per decade between 1951 and 2004. However, longer growing seasons are not uniformly good. In the south of France, apricot trees now flower one to three weeks earlier than in past decades, putting them at risk for spring frost and bud necrosis.

Arid regions have tended to become warmer and drier, and wet regions have become even wetter. As a result, crop yields have grown in wet regions but shrunk in arid regions. The loss of crops due to a reduction in rainfall is intensified by the expansion of insect ranges and increased forest fires. Another hazard in the drier areas is **desert-ification**, the process by which dry air evaporates moisture from the soil and the land turns to desert. Where possible, farmers in arid lands increase the amount of irrigation, but where this is not possible, land that was once farmable is lost.

More extreme weather events are affecting agriculture, even in the developed nations. In the United Kingdom, drought has caused farmers to increase the percentage of crops they irrigate. The European

An extremely dry village in sub-Saharan Africa. *(peeterv/iStockphoto)*

heat wave of 2003 decreased crop yields by up to 30% in some nations, including Greece, Portugal, Italy, and especially France.

Little is known about the effects of climate change on subsistence agriculture. In the Sahel in sub-Saharan Africa, where farming is extremely marginal, higher temperatures and lower rainfall have reduced the chance that the strains of plants that are currently being grown are able to complete their life cycle. Some rice-growing regions in Southeast Asia appear to be undergoing a slight decrease in productivity.

FORESTS

The Intergovernmental Panel on Climate Change (IPCC) says that up to one-third of forests have already been affected by climate change. On average, forest productivity has increased slightly. Thriving and expanding forests absorb more CO_2, which is a negative feedback for global warming. Of course, enough tropical forests are being cut down that this positive effect is more than made up for.

Regional warming has had a devastating effect on forests in the Southwestern United States. Temperature increases coupled with a multiyear drought have been blamed for the largest loss of trees in a single location ever recorded. More than 45 million Piñon pines (*Pinus cembroides*), a stubby, nut-bearing tree, have died in New Mexico, where the plant is the state tree. The direct cause is the Piñon bark beetle (*Ips confuses*), but scientists say that higher temperatures are really to blame. This is because the spread of beetles is slowed by frost, but now that there are fewer frosts, the beetles are able to move into areas that were once inhospitable. Bark beetles are in Arizona's ponderosa pine forests, in Utah's spruces, and in Colorado's Douglas firs. In Alaska and British Columbia, 14 million acres (56,660 square km) of spruce have been killed by bark beetles.

"It's the type of thing we can expect more of with global warming," Professor David Breshears of the University of Arizona told *National Geographic News* in December 2005. "There is reason to believe other systems could get whacked the way the Southwest did."

Other diseases are ravaging western forests. Warmer temperatures allow the mountain pine beetle (*Dendroctonus ponderosae*) to complete its life cycle in one year rather than its previous two. Consequently, the beetles have increased in population, which has resulted in an increase in pine blister rust (*Cronartium ribicola*) in Rocky Mountain forests. The rust is a fungus transmitted by the beetles. Trees that are damaged or killed by bark beetles or pine blister rust are far more susceptible to the spread of forest fires.

Due to high ocean temperatures in the Caribbean and Atlantic basins and to ongoing deforestation of the Amazon rain forest, in 2005 the Amazon basin began the longest and worst drought since record keeping began. In some areas, water levels have dropped so low that the communities that depend on streams for transportation are completely isolated. Crops rot because they cannot be transported to market, and children cannot get to school. People living on the world's largest river are unable to find fresh water to drink. Fish die in the shallow water due to lack of oxygen, killing freshwater dolphins and other predators, and forcing people to depend on government food packages. Because streams also remove human waste, when the streams dry up, the resulting sewage backup raises fears of cholera and other waterborne illnesses. In the remaining stagnant pools, mosquitoes breed in increasing numbers, which has the potential to raise malaria levels in local populations.

Longer-term drought causes trees to die and become fuel for fires, which the Amazon has recently experienced. In the Western United States, warmer temperatures and earlier springs have caused an increase in the number, duration, and destructiveness of wildfires since the mid-1980s. Studies show that the cause of the fires was

Trees killed by bark beetle in the San Bernardino Mountains of California. The trees were weakened by drought, ozone, and years of fire exclusion and ecological change. *(CDF— California Department of Forestry)*

increased spring and summer temperatures and earlier snowmelt. Similar changes in wildfire increases have been seen in other parts of the Americas.

WRAP-UP

The effects of climate change are already apparent in living systems. Plants and animals are changing their ranges and the timing of their life cycles. As a result, some populations have expanded, some have decreased, and some have just shifted. If these strategies do not work, the organisms will die out locally, or the species may even become extinct. The loss of a species that is important in a food web, such as krill, can have repercussions throughout an ecosystem. The consequences of warming that have been seen so far are just the beginning of the changes that are predicted to come as temperatures continue to rise.

PART THREE

A WARMER FUTURE

Future Consequences of Global Warming

T he scientific consensus is that global warming is now under way. It is now necessary to determine how much, when, and what the consequences will be. As Dr. Robert Watson, then Chairman of the Intergovernmental Panel on Climate Change (IPCC), said in 2001, "The overwhelming majority of scientific experts, whilst recognizing that scientific uncertainties exist, nonetheless believe that human-induced climate change is already occurring and that future change is inevitable."

With the use of climate models, scientists are attempting to develop scenarios that predict the magnitude and timing of climate change.

FUTURE CLIMATE MODELS

To understand future climate scenarios, scientists construct complex climate models. Good climate models take into account paleoclimate data, thermal inertia, the effects of oceanic and atmospheric currents, and the cooling effects of sulfate aerosols, among many other factors.

Complex models require the use of very powerful computers to make these calculations.

Climate models have many uncertainties: Among the most important of them is the difficulty of predicting how humans will behave in the future. The models cannot predict, for example, how much carbon people will emit into the atmosphere. Will CO_2 emissions increase at the same rate they have for the past decade? Or will they increase at an even higher rate due to improvements in lifestyles in the developing world (and even further improvements in the developed world)? Or might they decrease due to conscious changes in lifestyle or technology? Because human behavior is unpredictable, climatologists construct models using different estimates for these numbers, ranging from conservative to extreme. For example, a climatologist might input an annual reduction in carbon emissions into a conservative model or allow CO_2 emissions to grow rapidly using an extreme model. After the calculations are made, the results will be very different.

Models of future climate look at the effects on the Earth's system of various increases in greenhouse gas levels or in temperature. The simplest of them are called **commitment models**, which predict the responses that are inevitable due to greenhouse gases that have already been added to the atmosphere. A commitment model predicts the amount of warming that will occur as thermal inertia is overcome, even if people stop adding greenhouse gases to the atmosphere. For example, the temperature commitment for greenhouse gases released as of 2000 is a rise of between 0.9° and 1.8°F (0.5° and 1.0°C) by 2100. Commitment models are extremely unrealistic because they assume that people will immediately cease emitting greenhouse gases. Their value is in providing a baseline picture of the inevitable changes to come.

Many models of future climate assume that greenhouse gas levels will be stabilized at a temperature or a CO_2 level that society chooses. These models require that people choose a value and actively reduce greenhouse gas emissions to reach it. Some modelers use a doubling of atmospheric CO_2 from its preindustrial value of 280 ppm. A recent report says that a CO_2 value of 560 ppm will cause average global temperature to rise up to 5°F (2.8°C).

The doubling model does not take time into account, so there is no time frame for when this doubling will occur. To determine when this CO_2 level will be reached, a rate of change of CO_2 values must be figured into the model. One commonly used rate of change is an increase in CO_2 by an extra 1% per year. In this model, CO_2 doubles over preindustrial values by about 2080. Indeed, a value of 560 ppm CO_2 by 2080 is not unlikely.

The business-as-usual model assumes that emissions will rise along the same trajectory they have been on for the past decade, and that there will be no efforts to reduce greenhouse gas emissions. At this rate, CO_2 emissions in 2015 will be 35% greater than they were in 2000, and in 2030 they will be 63% greater than they were in 2002. The business-as-usual model results in CO_2 levels over 600 ppm and a temperature increase of 0.9 to 3.6°F (0.5 to 2°C) by 2050. (Thermal inertia would keep the temperature from rising higher.) By 2100, CO_2 could reach 880 to 1,000 ppm, a level not seen for at least 30 million years, with a certain temperature rise of between 3.5 and 8°F (2 and 4.5°C) and a 10% chance of an even greater rise.

Most models stop at the year 2100 or at a doubling of CO_2, but one business-as-usual model by scientists at the Lawrence Livermore Laboratory in California was allowed to run out to 2300. This model calculated what would happen if people continued to use fossil fuels until the Earth's entire supply was exhausted. The model run began in 1870 and predicted a fairly accurate increase in temperature of 1.4°F (0.8°C) by 2000. By 2300, there was a quadrupling of CO_2 levels from preindustrial to 1,423 ppm, and global surface temperatures were 14.5°F (7.8°C) higher than today. Land and polar areas warmed more, with the most extreme warming of more than 36°F (20°C) taking place over the Arctic. The oceans absorbed a great deal of CO_2 and became more acidic, with the potential of harming marine life. As seawater temperature surged, much of the ocean's dissolved CO_2 was driven back into the atmosphere, which further enhanced warming. The most drastic changes came in the twenty-second century, when greenhouse gas emissions rates were the highest and the environmental changes—in precipitation, extent of sea ice, and other features—were the greatest. Ice and tundra gave way to forests, and Northern Hemisphere sea ice cover disappeared almost completely by 2150.

The study's lead author, Govindasamy Bala, recognizes some weaknesses in the model but says that correcting the weaknesses would actually make the situation more drastic. The model assumes that soil and living biomass on land are carbon sinks but does not take into account a few factors such as the clearing of forests. In a 2006 press release about his study, Bala said, "We definitely know we are going to warm over the next 300 years. In reality, we may be worse off than we predict."

In the alternative scenario, people quickly and severely limit greenhouse gas emissions. CO_2 emissions level off by the end of this decade, slowly decline for a few decades, and begin to decrease rapidly by mid-century. Depending on the magnitude of the greenhouse gas emission reduction, this model predicts an increase of less than 2°F (1.1°C) this century.

The models discussed above are global models, but local models can be constructed as well. Global models leave out some very important information. A good example is the effect of global warming on the Arctic. A global average temperature increase of 5°F (2.8°C) means a one- or two-degree increase at the equator but a 12°F (6.7°C) increase at the North Pole. This has profound implications for melting sea ice and ice caps, for polar ecosystems, and for the climate system due to the positive feedback of reduced albedo.

Global dimming may be a larger factor in the accuracy of climate models than anyone realized until recently. Most climate models use the link between CO_2 levels and past temperature to predict how temperature will respond to future CO_2 levels. But scientists now say that warming in recent decades has been partially counteracted by global dimming. In that case, climate models consistently underestimate the temperature effects of rising CO_2 if global dimming is reduced (due to pollution reductions). For example, when a climate model that predicts a 9°F (5°C) temperature increase by the end of the century has a reduction in global dimming factored in, the predicted temperature increase

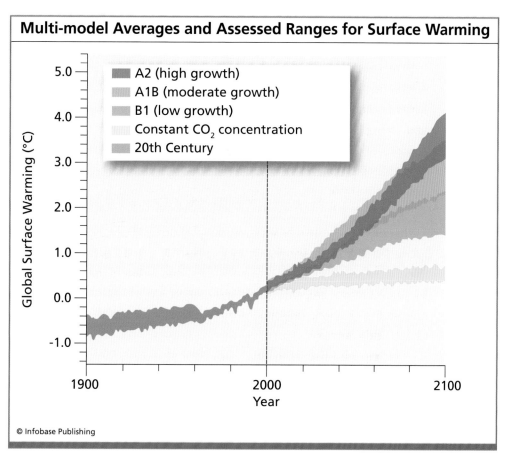

Multi-model Averages and Assessed Ranges for Surface Warming

Legend:
- A2 (high growth)
- A1B (moderate growth)
- B1 (low growth)
- Constant CO_2 concentration
- 20th Century

Y-axis: Global Surface Warming (°C)
X-axis: Year (1900, 2000, 2100)

© Infobase Publishing

Different models of climate change predict different temperatures by 2100, depending on whether or how much greenhouse gas emissions are restricted. The averages of the different models are included in the gray area; the colored shading encompasses projected growth ranges for the twenty-first century.

rises to 18°F (10°C). Therefore, unless greenhouse gas emissions are also curbed, a decrease in air pollution will increase global warming.

While the timing and magnitude of changes due to rising temperature cannot be known with certainty, climatologists agree that all models point in the same direction. Another point of agreement is that climate change will not continue to be gradual; when thresholds are broken, climate will change rapidly.

CLIMATE CONSEQUENCES BY TEMPERATURE

The IPCC's Fourth Assessment (IPCC-4) report, from 2007, shows the responses that can be expected for various increases in temperature above 1990 levels:

- ⊕ Up to 1.8°F (1°C): Some ecosystem shifts; most coral reefs bleached; some increases in global agricultural production potential, but reduced yields at lower latitudes; increases in severe storms
- ⊕ From 1.8 to 3.6°F (1 to 2°C): About one-quarter of species lost from current range; further increases in global agricultural production potential but further yield reduction at lower latitudes; coastal flooding; increased water stress in dry areas, with increased risk to human health; increased frequency and intensity of drought; increased heat waves
- ⊕ For 3.6 to 5.4°F (2 to 3°C): Most of tundra and about half of boreal forest area disappears; about one-third of species lost from current range; all coral reefs bleached; global agricultural production potential peaks, bringing hunger to populations in lower latitudes; 1 billion people become water stressed
- ⊕ For 5.4 to 7.2°F (3 to 4°C): Global decreases in agricultural production potential; large numbers additionally at risk of hunger; up to one-third of global population water stressed; widespread deglaciation and disintegration of West Antarctic Ice Sheet; further increased intensity and frequency of fire, drought, and storms
- ⊕ For 7.2 to 9.0°F (4 to 5°C): Decreases in agricultural production potential at higher latitudes, as well as further decreases at lower latitudes; too expensive to protect many areas from flooding; frequency of hot days much greater, many locations very difficult to live in; weakening and shutdown of some ocean currents, including Atlantic meridional overturning

⊕ For 9.0 to 10.8°F (5 to 6°C): Widespread species extinction.

The following sections describe in more detail what climate models predict for the future as temperature rises.

TEMPERATURE PATTERNS

Temperatures will rise as atmospheric greenhouse gas levels increase, but temperature increases will lag behind greenhouse gas levels due to thermal inertia. Temperatures will not increase uniformly around the globe: Most lands will warm more than the oceans due to the thermal inertia of the seas; the Northern Hemisphere will warm more than the Southern because it is mostly land; and the polar regions will warm much more than the rest of the planet due to the transition of ice to liquid water.

WATER CYCLE

The water cycle will continue to intensify. Precipitation will decrease in drier areas, including in many mid-continental areas, and increase in wetter areas. Rainfall will decline in some locations in the summer, which will harm crop yields, increase forest fires, and increase water stress. Currently, about 1.7 billion people live in countries that are water stressed: By 2025, that number will likely grow to 5 billion. Droughts will become longer and fiercer, making many marginal regions difficult or impossible to inhabit, including the western United States, northern China, and southern Africa. Deserts will become drier, and the Asian monsoon will be enhanced but will likely become more variable.

ARCTIC

The Arctic will continue to melt. As ice is lost, animals such as polar bears and seals will become greatly reduced in number or will go extinct. Many scientists say that unless drastic changes are made, the Arctic as it has been for the past several centuries is doomed.

OCEANS

The oceans will experience large temperature rises, and ocean life will move poleward where possible. A dramatic impact will be seen in coral reefs, which may die out almost completely in the next 50 years. A temperature rise of 1.8°F (1°C) is predicted to lead to extensive irreversible coral bleaching, particularly in years when other ocean warming events such as El Niño are superimposed. Between 2030 and 2050, the world's most magnificent coral reef, Australia's Great Barrier Reef, will experience annual bleaching due to warmer temperatures and other stresses such as higher sea level. Losing coral reefs does not only mean losing a unique and beautiful ecosystem and the food sources it contains. Coral reefs are nurseries for many types of fish. If reefs die, commercial fisheries, many of which are already currently being overfished, may collapse.

Ocean **acidification**, the decrease in oceanic pH, will decrease the ability of organisms to make carbonate shells, and existing carbonate shells will dissolve. This effect will be seen first in the cooler waters of the polar regions because cold water absorbs more CO_2 gas. Warmer waters will acidify later, and coral reefs will be affected. Dr. Richard Norris of Scripps Institution of Oceanography in California, who has worked on foram chemistry from the Paleocene-Eocene Thermal Maximum (PETM), calculates that the amount of carbon needed to create the effects seen on deep sea life in the PETM is 2,500 to 4,000 gigatons (Gt). Norris points out that, "The projected addition of fossil fuel CO_2 in the next couple hundred years is about 5000 Gt, which is comfortably enough to completely acidify the ocean right up to the surface waters."

Taking into account thermal inertia, thermal expansion, and glacial melting, the IPCC predicts a sea level rise of between 7 and 32 inches (18 and 81 cm) by the end of the century (by contrast, sea level rose between 6 and 9 inches [15 and 23 cm] in the twentieth century) and that the seas will rise for at least 1,000 years. Many coastal ecosystems are hemmed in by human development and will be unable to move inland. Human developments themselves will be lost as storms do their damage farther inland, atop higher seas. A report by the Heinz Center for Science, Economics, and the Environment in Washington, D.C., states that in the United States, rising seas will make at least 25% of the houses within 500 feet (150 m) of the coast (more than 350,000 total) uninhabitable by 2060. A one-foot (30-cm) sea level rise in Florida would cause the loss of 100 feet (30 m) of beaches. By 2080, rising seas could force hundreds of millions of people, particularly in nations without the resources to protect their coastlines, to abandon low-lying coastal areas.

Rising seas will force residents to step up engineering and beach replenishment projects. As this becomes more difficult and expensive, some coastal areas will be abandoned. As a preventative measure, coastal geologists recommend building farther inland from the coast.

AGRICULTURE

Initially high temperatures and changing precipitation patterns may increase crop yields in mid to high latitudes and decrease them in low latitudes. But, eventually, hotter and drier conditions will decrease agricultural productivity in higher latitudes as well. Locations that become drier will rely more on irrigation. Countries that are already straining to supply enough water for their people and crops may not succeed. As a result, famine may become more common in places such as sub-Saharan Africa and, ultimately, many other regions. Warmer temperatures are predicted to increase the range of plant diseases and parasites.

Some models predict that CO_2 doubling will lead to a 35% loss in agricultural regions of the United States and quadrupling will result in a 60% loss. The North American breadbasket will move from the midwestern United States into Canada. Similar changes will occur all over the world, resulting in a total loss of current cropland of 10 to 50%, and a decline in the global yield of key food crops of between

10% and 70%. Although climate may become suitable for agriculture at high latitudes, moving farms poleward where there is now tundra is not a reasonable solution. Crops need good soil, which takes tens or hundreds of years to develop. Short-term adaptations to warmer temperatures, such as increased irrigation, could put off these problems for a time.

EXTREME WEATHER

Climate models predict that extreme weather events will become more common, among them intense rainstorms, flooding, heat waves, droughts, and violent storms. There are two reasons for this: Many weather events are caused by high temperatures, and warm air holds more moisture than cool air, allowing more chance for precipitation. SST will also rise, bringing about more El Niño events and the consequent floods and droughts.

Heat waves will increase the most in quantity and severity in warm regions but will also be more common in cooler areas. Commenting on the 2003 European heat wave, British Prime Minister Tony Blair said in 2004, "It is calculated that such a summer is a one in about 800-year event. On the latest modeling, climate change means that as soon as the 2040s at least one year in two is likely to be even warmer than 2003."

Climate models of the years 2080 to 2099 indicate that both Chicago and Paris will have more heat waves, 25% and 31%, respectively; and their length will increase 64% and 52%, respectively. Precipitation events will also increase, although in some regions summers will be a lot drier and droughts will become more common.

Researchers have conflicting ideas on whether global warming will increase the number of hurricanes. Warmer SST will allow more storms to form, but higher air temperatures will increase the wind shear between the lower and upper atmosphere, causing many developing storms to be decapitated. Several researchers agree that warmer SST could increase the number of storms. A model by Matthew Huber and Ryan L. Sriver of Purdue University, published in *Geophysical*

Research Letters in 2006, indicates that a one-quarter-degree increase in average global temperature will double the intensity and frequency of hurricanes. Kerry Emanuel and Michael E. Mann at Pennsylvania State University attribute the recent rise in hurricane activity to increasing SST. They suggest that the most recent period of low hurricane activity was not due to natural variations but due to global dimming, and that a further decrease in aerosol pollution could increase hurricane activity even more.

The hurricanes of the future will certainly be more intense. A summary of 1,200 simulations, published in the *Journal of Climate* in 2004, showed that rising levels of greenhouse gases could triple the number of Category 5 hurricanes. Climate models show that by 2080, each hurricane will be about one-half point higher on the Saffir-Simpson scale than the current average, with a resulting 20% increase in rainfall. A study by the United States Federal Emergency Management Agency (FEMA) found that a one-foot (30 cm) sea level rise would increase flood damage by hurricanes by 36% to 58%.

HUMAN HEALTH

Increases in extreme weather events will take a toll on human health; for example, an increase in heat waves will trigger a rise in heat-related deaths. Losses of agricultural productivity and clean water supplies will also be felt. By 2030, climate-related deaths by malnutrition and diarrhea will increase noticeably.

Microbes are held in check by colder winters and colder nights. Warmer temperatures will continue to allow diseases to expand their ranges, and increased food poisoning will strike the temperate regions as parasites spread. For example, ciguatera and other fish and shellfish poisoning will spread into the warmer seas. Heavy rainfall could increase outbreaks of waterborne disease; a recent example is the parasitic infections that sickened 400,000 people in Milwaukee in 1993 following the heaviest rainfall in a single month in 50 years.

The expansion in the range of insect pests from tropical and subtropical regions to temperate zones will spread the diseases they carry into places where they have never been before. Some of the diseases that are expected to proliferate are malaria, encephalitis, yellow fever, dengue fever, and cholera. The expansion of diseases into new areas has already taken place; for example, tick-borne encephalitis was unknown in Sweden until the mid-1980s. The warming of the Kenyan highlands may have allowed malaria to spread into the region in the past 20 years (although other factors, such as the banning of the pesticide DDT, may also be involved).

Extremely dry conditions also contribute to the spread of disease. The 1999 outbreak of West Nile virus in New York corresponded with a severe drought, while African dust caused by climate change has been linked to respiratory disease in the Caribbean.

WRAP-UP

Climate models show that as temperatures continue to rise, many of the predicted changes will be continuations of changes that have already taken place. Polar ice will continue to melt, and extreme weather events will continue to increase in frequency, for example. Diseases that are common in tropical areas will spread into temperate zones, affecting people in the developed nations as well as the developing ones.

Climate models predict the consequences of a doubling of CO_2 over preindustrial levels. In 2006, Kenneth Caldeira of the Department of Global Ecology at the Carnegie Institution said, "The doubled-CO_2 climate that scientists have warned about for decades is beginning to look like a goal we might attain if we work hard to limit CO_2 emissions, rather than the terrible outcome that might occur if we do nothing." The consequences of even higher temperatures are described in Chapter 10.

The Tipping Point

Climate scientists are becoming concerned about the speed at which temperatures are rising, and the consequences of global warming are being realized. James E. Hansen, director of the National Aeronautic and Space Administration's (NASA) Goddard Institute of Space Studies, said in 2006 that a temperature increases of 4°F (2.2°C) in this century would "imply changes that constitute practically a different planet." Hansen's statement suggests that climate may, in the next few decades, reach the point of no return: the place scientists call the **tipping point**, a concept that will be described in this chapter.

WHAT IS THE TIPPING POINT?

A toy car sitting on the flat above a steep slope can be inched slowly toward the slope for a time. Eventually, though, enough of the car's mass will be over the slope that the car will careen down the hill. The point when the car is about to head downhill, at which its downward momentum can no longer be stopped, is its tipping point. A system's tipping point is tied to its positive feedbacks.

Climate will reach the tipping point when catastrophic change becomes inevitable: When it reaches the point where it is too late to act. There are many tipping points along the way. The first will be when the first irreversible event occurs, but many others will follow it. Some climatologists say that the first tipping point will come in the next several decades if greenhouse gas emissions are not halved over the next 50 years.

This chapter describes some of the events that warming temperatures may push to their tipping point, just as the toy car was inched to its tipping point. The time frames of these events range from the coming decades to centuries or millennia. Each event has a different tipping point, and each is irreversible once that point is crossed, at least on a timescale that is meaningful for humans.

THE LOSS OF MAJOR ICE SHEETS AND RISING SEA LEVEL

When a glacier warms, the rate of melting increases because meltwater lubricates the glacier and causes it to slide more and melt faster. Once an ice sheet begins to break up, it may not stop until it has all melted away, or until the next ice age arrives.

Although no one can know what the tipping point for the Greenland ice sheet is, many scientists think it could be reached with a regional temperature increase of 5°F (2.7°C), which corresponds to a global increase of 2.7°F (1.5°C) above the present level. This magnitude of global increase could be reached through a doubling of CO_2 and could occur as early as 2080 or even sooner. After this tipping point is reached, thermal inertia would keep the ice sheet from melting abruptly. Eventually, though, the ice sheet would melt completely, raising the sea level about 23 feet (7 m).

Recent reports indicate that ice loss in Greenland is greatly accelerating. One study showed that melting in 2006 was twice as fast as in the previous five years. Greenland's ice mass has already decreased

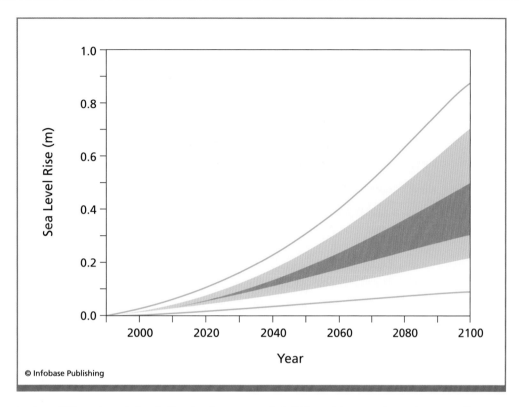

Just as different models of climate change predict different temperatures by 2100, they also predict different amounts of sea level rise. The area with the darkest shading in the center represents model averages; the lighter color introduces more uncertainty in ice-land interactions and thermal expansion of seawater; and the outlying lines envelope possible sea level rise taking all uncertainties into account except possible changes in the West Antarctic ice sheet.

by 50 cubic miles (208 cubic km), as more of the ice sheet melts and more giant icebergs calve into the sea. In early May 2006, temperatures were almost 20°F (11°C) above normal, just below freezing. Prolonged local heating of that magnitude could greatly hasten the loss of the Greenland ice sheet.

Models suggest that Antarctic ice sheets are more stable because they are larger and thicker. Nonetheless, the West Antarctic Ice Sheet (WAIS) is in the early stages of disintegrating, says the head of the British Antarctic Survey, Chris Rapley. In the report *Avoiding Dangerous*

Climate Change, Rapley wrote, "The last IPCC report characterized Antarctica as a slumbering giant in terms of climate change. I would say it is now an awakened giant. There is real concern." The total collapse of the WAIS could raise sea level by 16 feet (4.9 m).

The effect of all that melting, coupled with thermal expansion, would be an enormous sea level rise. The record of the geologic past suggests that during ice sheet collapse, the sea level can rise 16 feet (5 m) per century. A 20-foot (6-m) increase in sea level would inundate Seattle, portions of Manhattan, and the southern one-third of Florida (including Miami). According to former U.S. Vice President

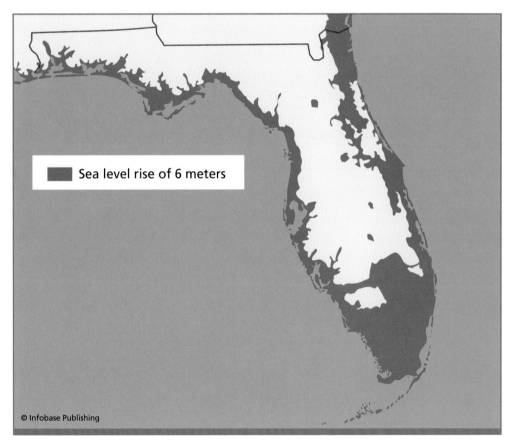

Sea level rise of 6 meters

© Infobase Publishing

A 20-foot (6-m) rise in sea level would drown the southern one-third and coastal areas of Florida and make regions that are now well inland vulnerable to ocean storms.

Al Gore's book *An Inconvenient Truth*, a 20-foot (6-m) rise in sea level will displace 20 million people in Beijing, China; 40 million in Shanghai, China; and 60 million in Calcutta, India, and Bangladesh.

The melting of ice sheets would be fairly slow because of thermal inertia, but history indicates what will happen once this melting occurs. When the average temperature was last 5°F (2.8°C) globally and 10°F (5.6°C) at the high latitudes, about 3 million years ago, sea level was 80 feet (24 m) above what it is today. A rise of that magnitude will partially or wholly inundate many regions, including San Francisco, New York, portions of Los Angeles, Washington D.C., and nearly all of Florida and the Gulf of Mexico coastal region. Globally, Tokyo, London, Beijing, and much of the Netherlands would be submerged.

AN ICE AGE FOR EUROPE

Global warming threatens oceanic currents that have been stable for thousands of years. Paradoxically, changing currents could cause Europe to cool at a time when most of the rest of the world is heating up. The prediction is for a scenario like the Younger Dryas, about 10,500 years ago, when an influx of freshwater into the North Atlantic slowed thermohaline circulation in the region.

The freshening of the North Atlantic during the Younger Dryas was due to a breached ice dam that allowed glacial meltwater to flood the surface ocean. Future freshening will be the result of increased rainfall, runoff from melting ice sheets, and a lessening of sea ice formation. Because this relatively light freshwater will not sink, Atlantic meridional overturning circulation in the North Atlantic will end or slow considerably.

North Atlantic surface water salinity has been decreasing for the past few decades. As a result, overturning circulation weakened by 30% between 1957 and 2004, according to a 2005 report in *Nature* by Harry Bryden and other scientists at the National Oceanography Center in Britain. Although the northward flow of the Gulf Stream is so far unchanged, about 20% less deep water appears to be traveling southward.

These observed changes are consistent with climate model predictions. Eventually, the continued influx of freshwater into the North Atlantic may slow or stop the pull of the equatorial Gulf Stream waters toward the north. If this occurs, temperatures in the British Isles and northern Europe will cool by about 5.4 to 12.6°F (3 to 5°C), which is comparable to the Little Ice Age of the sixteenth to eighteenth centuries.

The Younger Dryas, in addition to a more recent freeze that occurred 8,200 years ago, took hold over a decade or two and lasted for hundreds of years. While it clearly is possible for the salinity of the North Atlantic to reach a tipping point that slows or stops normal ocean circulation patterns, no one knows when this might next occur; there are many scientists who say that it is unlikely to occur at all. Still, Hans Joachim Schellnhuber, who directs Germany's Potsdam Institute for Climate Impact Research, has run multiple computer models that concluded in 2006 that there is a 50% chance that the Atlantic meridional circulation will collapse within 200 years.

SPECIES EXTINCTIONS

Throughout Earth history, species of plants and animals have gone extinct. This happens more often when conditions are difficult, such as they are after an asteroid impact or during a massive flood basalt eruption. Extinction rates are lower when conditions are more stable. In recent decades, species extinctions have risen to about 1,000 times the normal background rate. These extinctions are due mainly to human activities, primarily changes in land use. The conversion of tropical rain forests to ranchland, for example, results in a tremendous loss of species. In the future, warmer temperatures will destroy the delicate balance many species have with their environment, which will trigger their extinction. The loss of important species could cause entire ecosystems to collapse.

So far, the extinction of only one species has been directly attributed to global warming, and even then not all scientists agree that warming is entirely to blame. That species was the Monteverde Golden Toad

(*Bufo periglenes*), formerly found in a Costa Rican nature preserve called the Monteverde Cloud Forest. The extinction came suddenly, between 1987, when an American ecologist, Martha Crump, counted about 1,500 Golden Toads during mating season, and 1988, when she returned to find no breeding toads—and none have been found since.

Scientists blame the extinction on the chytrid fungus (*Batrachochytrium dendrobatidis*), which destroys the frogs' skin, ultimately killing them. Although the Monteverde and other Central American cloud forests are usually covered in mist, on sunny days the toads rid themselves of the fungus by basking in the sun and raising their temperatures above 86°F (30°C). However, warmer air temperatures increased the amount of cloud cover over the mountain. This reduced the amount of sunlight, so the toads could not raise their body temperatures high enough to kill off the fungus.

The chytrid fungus is responsible for population declines or extinctions in at least 100 species of amphibians in the United States, Central and South America, Europe, New Zealand, and Australia. Amphibian populations are plummeting globally; nearly one-third (1,856) of the 5,743 known amphibian species are threatened, and more than 100 have likely gone extinct since 1980, according to the Global Amphibian Assessment. Habitat destruction, pollution, and disease are taking an enormous toll, but global warming is a factor in many of these extinctions. As evidence, 78% to 83% of the known extinctions occurred in years that were unusually warm across the tropics. Like the Monteverde Golden Toad, several amphibian species were last seen in 1988, following a very hot 1987.

In the oceans, the extinction of phytoplankton due to acidification and rising temperatures could initiate a collapse of ocean ecosystems. This acidification will also harm larger organisms. A model published in *Nature* by James C. Orr and other scientists in September 2005 projected that organisms such as coral, shellfish, and sea stars could have trouble forming their shells in Southern Ocean surface waters as soon as 2050 and in a larger area by 2100. Warmer seawater temperatures would lower the amount of oxygen, which would also be detrimental to ocean life.

Warmer temperatures are already causing some species to move to new locations, as described in Chapter 8. Studies show that land plants and animals will need to move poleward 60 to 90 miles (100 to 150 km) or upward 500 feet (150 m) for each 1.8°F (1°C) rise in global temperature. Native species may be driven out of the area by more heat-tolerant nonnative species. If a species cannot move or overcome competition from nonnative species, it will become locally extinct. If the species has a small distribution, or if it experiences problems throughout its range, it will go extinct. As a result, **biodiversity**—the number of species in a given habitat—will decline.

Some species have so far been successful at moving to more favorable climate conditions, as the Parmesan and Yohe study showed. However, in a 2006 article in the *New York Review of Books*, NASA's James Hansen said that during the time the scientists chronicled range changes in these species, average temperatures moved poleward at more than eight times that pace (35 miles, or 56 km, per decade). Species are not keeping up, and this could cause future population declines. Also, if projected temperature increases follow the business-as-usual model, temperatures will move toward the poles at double the current rate, at least 70 miles (113 km) per decade. Most species will not be able to migrate this fast, which will likely result in many extinctions. The species that are most at risk are those species that live in the polar regions and on mountaintops: They would have nowhere to move.

During Earth history, many organisms seemed to be able to adapt to times of rapid climate change and did not go extinct. But higher temperatures are not the only stress humans are placing on the other inhabitants of Earth. Organisms cannot move in response to changing climate if they run into farms, urban sprawl, or pollution. In his book *The Weather Makers*, Tim Flannery calculates that in a business-as-usual scenario, and taking into account the other stresses human are causing, about 60% of Earth's species could go extinct. Using the alternative scenario, in which people significantly reduce greenhouse gas emissions, the number is 20%. Of course, these numbers cannot be established with any certainty.

Says NASA's Hansen, "Life will survive, but it will do so on a transformed planet. For all foreseeable human generations, it will be a far more desolate world than the one in which civilization developed and flourished during the past several thousand years."

Even scientists making the direst predictions of species extinction take a longer term view. A mass extinction caused by climate change will wipe out many of the species currently on the planet, but ultimately the Earth will stabilize, and new species will evolve that are adapted to the new conditions. Although some ecosystems and organisms will suffer greatly, humans are as dependent on the status quo as any species, so they will likely suffer as much as any organism.

CLIMATE REFUGEES

Refugees are people who have nowhere to go. Traditionally, refugees have been displaced due to war or political persecution. Now a new type of refugee is being proposed: **Environmental refugees**, those who are displaced from their homes by environmental changes. Although no organization yet recognizes them, they may already number 25 million. A large subcategory of environmental refugees is **climate refugees**—people who are displaced by increases in extreme weather events, sea level rise, or any other effect of climate change.

Climate refugees are beginning to leave the small, inhabited islands of the southwestern Pacific Ocean. Many of these islands are low-lying coral atolls that may rise only a few feet above sea level. Rising seas and storm surges damage homes and reduce the atoll residents' ability to support themselves. According to the Red Cross in 2005, the number of people in the southwestern Pacific that have been affected by weather-related disasters has increased 65 times in the past 30 years. Many of these people have already become, or soon will become, climate refugees.

Residents of the Carteret Islands are the first refugees being driven from their homes by rising seas. These six tiny horseshoe-shaped coral atolls are part of Papua New Guinea. The nearly 1,000 inhabitants have been trying to save their home for 20 years by planting mangroves and building seawalls. Despite their efforts, high tides and storm surges wash over the island, destroying homes and coconut palms and contaminating crops and freshwater supplies. Waves have broken off small pieces of the coral atolls. Scientists predict that the islands will be totally submerged by 2015. In 2005, the Papua New Guinea government decided to move 10 families at a time to a new, larger island home on Bougainville, a four-hour boat trip away.

The Carteret Islanders are a small group. Other locations, with bigger populations, could create many more climate refugees, which makes for additional problems. Densely populated Indonesia could lose about 2,000 islands by 2030. Extremely remote Tuvalu, the world's second smallest nation (after Vatican City), with only 11,600 residents, is already losing people. Many of the residents of Tuvalu's nine islands have already left their homes for New Zealand, where they try to maintain their unique culture while working and living among the New Zealanders. Although for many years Tuvaluans have left their islands because of overcrowding or in search of better jobs, island flooding due to climate change is increasingly cited as a motivation for evacuation.

Some Tuvaluans are fighting to protect their island homes. The islanders have even sent an ambassador to the United Nations to tell the world of their plight. Tuvaluan ambassador Enele Sopoaga told writer Alexandra Berzon, for a 2006 article, "Tuvalu is Drowning," in the online magazine *Salon*, "Tuvaluans want to live in their own islands forever. To relocate is a shortsighted solution, an irresponsible solution. We're not dealing here with Tuvalu only. All of the low-lying island coastal areas are going to be affected."

Island nation residents are not the only ones who have to worry about becoming climate refugees. Enormous numbers of climate refugees will come from developing nations, too. Climate change could create 250 million refugees in China, 150 million in India, and 120 million in Bangladesh, for example. As climate refugees are displaced in ever-increasing numbers, the question of what to do with them will be more crucial. New Zealand has agreed to take 75 Tuvaluans per year on a special permit, and others have gone to Australia or other

Children waiting out a flood at their home on Tuvalu. (© *Gary Braasch, from the book* Earth Under Fire: How Global Warming Is Changing the World, *University of California Press, 2007*)

island nations. But what happens when the numbers of climate refugees seeking asylum rises into the millions? Indeed, the third Intergovernmental Panel on Climate Change (IPCC) report in 2001 states there may be 150 million environmental refugees by 2050.

Some people say that the nations most responsible for climate change should take most of the refugees, and suggest that the obligations should be proportional to the nation's impact. In other words, the United States, which produced around 30% of the CO_2 emissions during the twentieth century, would take about 30% of climate refugees, which would be as many as 250,000 to 750,000 people a year. Andrew Simms, head of the climate change program at the New Economics Foundation, wrote in the *Guardian* in 2003 that the advantage to this strategy would be that "Creating new legal obligations to accept environmental refugees would help ensure that industrialized countries accept the consequences of their choices."

But the United States will not just need to take on foreign refugees—it will already have many of its own. Sea level rise will eventually make much of the Gulf of Mexico and South Florida coasts, as well as many coastal cities, uninhabitable. Eventually, as many as 50 million people could be flooded out. The New Orleans residents displaced by Hurricane Katrina could be considered to be climate refugees, although they are not the nation's first: the Dust Bowl of the mid- to late-1930s, which created over 500,000 refugees, was partly caused by a massive drought.

HUMAN CIVILIZATION

The impacts of climate change will strike developing nations earlier and harder than developed nations. Part of this is due to location because developed countries tend to be in the middle and middle-high latitudes, so they will see less impact for a time. Developing nations have large populations with greater immediate exposure to risk. Most of these countries do not have the money to prepare for the anticipated effects of climate change such as rising sea level or to recover from extreme weather events such as storms. According to the IPCC, by 2100, the coastal regions of developing nations will have 30 times more people displaced and 12 times as much area inundated, and will need to spend three times the cost for flood protection when compared with the developed nations. The wealthier nations of the world may come to the aid of the poorer ones for a time, but the costs may eventually become too great.

In developed countries, the costs of climate change may be masked for a time. The effects of increasing the amount of land that receives irrigation or simply increasing the amount of water for irrigation will not readily be noticed. For a time, private insurance will pay for damage due to extreme climate events. Events such as the heat wave of 2003 in Western Europe and Hurricane Katrina in 2005 in the United

States may be seen as isolated events that are not due to a single over-arching cause.

Ultimately, though, the costs of dealing with climate change all over the world will be very high. Swiss Re, the world's second largest insurer, estimates that global warming could cost $150 billion each year in the next 10 years, including $30 to $40 billion in insurance claims. With that much money in claims, private insurers will be forced to increase costs or decrease coverage in high-risk areas. When private insurers pull out, governments and individuals are left to repair the damage. This effect is already being seen in coastal Florida as insurers drastically increase rates or refuse to insure residents of hurricane-prone areas.

Positive feedbacks could keep the Earth in a warming trend for thousands or tens of thousands of years, as has happened in the geologic past. While such a long period of time is just a blip for the planet, it is potentially devastating for human society. The changes in climate will be far greater than anything seen during the course of human evolution, and while humans are smart and adaptable, it is unlikely that human civilization could survive unaltered. Just a small decrease in global food production or water availability could lead to famine, water scarcity, or political unrest—for several billion people.

Tim Flannery, in his 2006 book *The Weather Makers*, stated, "If humans pursue a business-as-usual course for the first half of this century, I believe the collapse of civilization due to climate change becomes inevitable."

While some climate scientists disagree with Flannery's "Chicken Little" tactic of screaming "the sky is falling," few climatologists would disagree that big changes for human society are ahead, unless big changes in greenhouse gas emissions are made very soon.

WRAP-UP

This chapter describes the extreme consequences of warming temperatures. None of these dire predictions is inevitable, but all are possible if greenhouse gas emissions continue to rise unchecked. Each of these events has a tipping point, although the tipping point for each is different. Each tipping point, if passed, will have dire effects on human civilization, which relies heavily on the status quo for agriculture, development, technology, and other aspects of its existence. With so much at stake, the actions people take now are crucial.

PART FOUR

APPROACHING THE CLIMATE CHANGE PROBLEM

Human Response

Climate scientists say that human activities are responsible for rising greenhouse gas emissions, increasing temperatures, and the climate-related changes Earth is now experiencing. The changes seen are consistent with climate model predictions. Now that the problem has been identified and agreed on, these scientists are increasingly calling for society to take action. The longer people wait to make the necessary changes, the more drastic those changes will need to be.

According to NASA's James Hansen, in a 2006 article in *The New York Review of Books*, "Our children, grandchildren, and many more generations will bear the consequences of choices that we make in the next few years."

WHY SHOULD PEOPLE PROTECT CLIMATE?

The climate has been warmer at various times in the geologic past. Even so, oceans continued to circulate while storms stormed, landscapes changed, and life flourished—Earth was in balance. This balance was different from today, but just as viable. So why should people attempt to maintain the climate as it is today?

One reason lies in peoples' relationship to the biosphere. In the geologic past, organisms adapted to changing climate biologically or behaviorally; and if they failed to adapt, they went extinct. When climate change was especially rapid, more species suffered, but many managed to make it through. Extinctions, whether from climate change or other causes, opened up the biosphere for new species to evolve. Scientists predict that the current greenhouse warming could cause the extinction of as many as 60% of Earth's species. This large number is due to the stress people are putting on the biosphere in other ways, primarily by changing how land is used and overharvesting resources. Although the human experience would be poorer without polar bears, condors, beluga whales, and monarch butterflies, life would survive; and in the long run, new species would evolve.

But if temperatures go higher than ever seen in human history, people will bear the brunt of the changes. Agriculture, technology, and urban development have advanced radically during the past centuries while climate has remained relatively mild and reasonably predictable. Without a stable climate, the social structures and systems built by humans will be endangered. And with more than 6.5 billion people on the planet, this possibility is extremely serious.

Andrew Revkin, a science journalist at *The New York Times*, said in 2006, "In fact, the planet has nothing to worry about from global warming. A hot, steamy earth would be fine for most forms of life. Earth and its biological veneer are far more resilient than human societies, particularly those still mired in poverty or pushed to the margins of the livable. Only we humans have to be concerned, and species like polar bears that, like the poorest people, are pushed to an edge—in the bear's case the tenuous ecosystem built around coastal sea ice."

MOVING PEOPLE TO ACTION

Scientists and supportive political leaders are outlining the actions that must be taken to avoid a horrific future caused by rapid climate change. They advocate two types of responses: **mitigation**, which means making the changes that are coming less severe by reducing greenhouse gas emissions, and **adaptation**, which means altering human behaviors to adjust to those changes that are inevitable.

Motivating political leaders and people in general to take action on climate change is difficult. In a 2004 speech, British Prime Minister Tony Blair, one of the foremost advocates for reducing greenhouse gas emissions, pointed out the two major problems with getting people and governments on board: First, the effects of climate change will not be fully realized for years or decades, making it difficult for political leaders, who are tied to election cycles, to take up the cause: "In other words," Blair said, "there is a mismatch in timing between the environmental and electoral impact." Second, any action taken must be international: "commonly agreed and commonly followed through." Getting agreement from political leaders on climate change has proven to be extremely difficult, as will be discussed later in this chapter.

SETTING LIMITS

Assuming action will be taken, what should be the first step? Some leaders recommend choosing a temperature increase above which society will not allow itself to go and reducing greenhouse gases emissions so that global temperature does not exceed that value.

The authors of the report *Avoiding Dangerous Climate Change*, published by the Tyndall Centre for Climate Change Research in the United Kingdom in 2005, suggest that to avoid dangerous climate change, the temperature rise should not exceed 3.6°F (2°C) above preindustrial levels. Their models show that keeping atmospheric CO_2 below 400 ppm would safely achieve this goal, but because 2006 levels were already above 380 ppm, that goal is virtually unattainable. If CO_2 levels are kept below 450 ppm, there is a 50% chance of keeping temperatures below the target value. The strategy suggested by Rachel Warren, one of the report's authors, is for CO_2 emissions to peak no later than 2025 and then come down by 2.6% per year. The CEO of British Petroleum, John Browne, has suggested a CO_2 stabilization target of about 560 ppm, twice the preindustrial level. Many scientists think that to keep greenhouse warming in check, CO_2 emissions must be cut in half over the next 50 years.

THE KYOTO PROTOCOL

The world's first coordinated response to the climate change problem was the Kyoto Protocol, an international treaty seeking "stabilization of greenhouse gas concentrations in the atmosphere at a level that would prevent dangerous anthropogenic interference with the climate system." The treaty was negotiated in Kyoto, Japan, in December 1997. After ratification by nearly every nation on Earth, it took effect in February 2005.

Kyoto regulates the greenhouse gases CO_2, methane, nitrous oxide, sulfur hexafluoride, HFCs, and PFCs. Under the protocol, 35 industrialized countries are obliged to reduce their greenhouse gas emissions by 5.2% below 1990 levels by sometime between 2008 and 2012. This value is 29% below what these nations' emissions would likely be without the reductions.

Kyoto's rules call for emissions reductions by an internationally agreed upon cap-and-trade program. Each nation's greenhouse gas emissions "cap" is set by the United Nations Framework Convention on Climate (UNFCC). These cap levels are based on the nation's size and the state of its economy: For instance, at this time, the cap is an 8% reduction from 1990 emissions for the European Union, a 6% reduction for Japan, a 0% reduction for Russia, plus permitted increases of 8% for Iceland.

With these caps, participating nations are then allowed to "trade" emissions credits amongst themselves. A country that will exceed its limit can buy credits from a country that will not use all of its credits. The trading scheme provides financial incentive for countries to meet and even exceed their targets. At this time Russia, which has far lower greenhouse gas than in 1990 due to an economic downturn and has also easily achieved increases in efficiency, is selling credits for hundreds of millions of dollars to countries that are not yet able to reach their targets. Russia receives much needed money, and all participants have an economic incentive to improve their energy efficiency.

Developing countries are at this time exempt from greenhouse gas emissions reductions because they have historically contributed a very small share of emissions. In addition, their per capita emissions are still relatively low, and they still have significant social needs. Nonetheless, Kyoto requires that developed nations assist developing ones by paying for and providing technology for climate-related studies and projects. Countries are also rewarded credits for protecting forests and other carbon dioxide sinks.

Unfortunately, Kyoto has many flaws, the most glaring being the countries that are not bound by it. The United States, which produced 21% of the total greenhouse gas emissions in 2000 and would have a cap of 7% below 1990 emissions, refused to sign because politicians feared that emissions restrictions would slow down the nation's economic growth. Although the nation engages in voluntary cutbacks, by 2005 greenhouse gas emissions of the United States were 19%

Cap-and-Trade Programs

Cap-and-trade programs are a popular, market-based approach for encouraging entities such as businesses, cities, or countries to reduce emissions. A neutral body sets an emissions cap for each program participant, usually based on the participant's past emissions. In most programs, the allowances can be used, traded to another participant, or banked for future use. Because allowances can be traded for cash, participants have a monetary incentive for developing emissions-saving technologies. If a participant exceeds its total allowances, it may be fined. In many programs, the emissions cap lessens over time until a permanent cap is reached.

A cap-and-trade program for sulfur oxide (SO_2) emissions has been extremely successful in reducing this acid rain–causing pollutant in the United States. When the permanent cap is reached, in 2010, emissions will be approximately 50% below 1980 levels. Cap-and-trade systems have been proposed for wider adoption for dealing with other pollution problems. However, some extremely toxic pollutants that might concentrate in a single area, such as mercury, are not well suited for such plans.

over what they would have been if it had adhered to its Kyoto limits. Australia also refused to sign, even though it was awarded an emissions increase of 10%. A small overall emitter, the nation was the largest per capita emitter in 2005, suggesting that there is plenty of room for improvement in Australia's energy efficiency. Although China's greenhouse gas contributions are enormous, the country is exempt from emissions reductions because it is a developing nation. In addition, many of the treaty's participants are not on target to meet their emissions goals.

Most importantly, climate scientists say that the Kyoto Protocol does not go nearly far enough. Even if all developed nations participated, the treaty would only result in a reduction in global temperature of between 0.04 and 0.5°F (0.02 and 0.28°C) by the year 2050. One climate model suggests that reductions of more than 40 times those required by Kyoto are needed to prevent atmospheric CO_2 concentrations from doubling during this century.

Defenders of the treaty say that it sets the stage for larger emissions limits in the future. The first commitment period ends in 2012, and negotiators are now working to make sure that another treaty will be ready to take its place and that emissions standards will be tougher. Ongoing talks emphasize developing new technologies and adapting to environmental changes that are already inevitable.

THE UNITED STATES AND GREENHOUSE GAS EMISSIONS

Many people and communities in the United States are frustrated by the lack of action being taken by the federal government and so are acting independently. A voluntary and legally binding cap-and-trade experiment, the Chicago Climate Exchange (CCX) has more than 175 members. These include globally important companies such as Ford and DuPont; the states of New Mexico and California; cities; farm bureaus; nongovernmental organizations; and universities, including Tufts. Together, these entities account for 4% of the annual emissions of the United States. The CCX is run partly as a trial so that a framework already will have been built when the government begins a nationwide compulsory cap-and-trade program—a development that most CCX participants believe is just a matter of time. CCX members make a voluntary but legally binding commitment to reduce emissions of six greenhouse gases by 6% by the end of 2010 below a baseline level created in the period covering 1998 to 2001. Members may also buy and sell credits and engage in other favorable activities such as reforestation projects. The participants are getting a head start by developing programs and technologies to reduce their own emissions.

Regions, states, and cities are developing their own emissions limitations programs, in part to pressure the federal government into developing an emissions reduction plan. Several states are implementing emissions trading plans. In August 2006, California became the first state to pass a cap-and-trade plan requiring the state's major industries to reduce greenhouse gas emissions by about 25% by 2020, in addition to the state's 2004 tailpipe emission reduction plan. As of May 2007, 522 mayors, representing 65 million citizens (including Seattle, New York, Los Angeles, San Francisco, Chicago, Boston, New Orleans, Minneapolis and many other localities), signed an agreement committing to take the following three actions:

- Strive to meet or beat the Kyoto Protocol targets in their own communities, through actions ranging from antisprawl land-use policies, to urban forest restoration projects, to public information campaigns.
- Urge their state governments, and the federal government, to enact policies and programs to meet or beat the greenhouse gas emission reduction target suggested for the United States in the Kyoto Protocol—a 7% reduction from 1990 levels by 2012.
- Urge the U. S. Congress to pass the bipartisan greenhouse gas reduction legislation, which would establish a national emission trading system.

A student group called Kyoto Now! is working to reduce emissions at American universities. The goal of People of the World Ratifying the Kyoto Protocol is to collect signatures from at least 50,000,000 individuals who support the Kyoto Protocol.

All of these local and regional efforts are good, but for an emissions reduction plan to really work, the plan must be international; and the United States must be a full participant for several reasons:

- Other nations are less likely to extend Kyoto (and certainly less likely to strengthen it) beyond 2012 without the participation of the world's historically largest greenhouse gas emitter.
- Companies and nations worldwide are less likely to invest the money needed to make the changes required to reduce emissions without the involvement of the large U.S. market.
- Companies would be more motivated to develop environmentally sound technologies if they could supply products to the world's largest economy.
- According to former British Prime Minister Tony Blair, the Chinese are unlikely to cooperate without the participation of the Americans, and their exploding emissions could overwhelm any gains made in emissions reductions by other nations.

WRAP-UP

Climate scientists advocate choosing an average global temperature increase above which society agrees not to go and reducing greenhouse gases emissions to keep global temperature from exceeding that value. To avoid dangerous climate change, emissions reductions need to be greater than those required by the Kyoto Protocol and will require the participation of all the nations of the world. In the absence of adequate government actions, some individuals, communities, and regions are beginning to take responsibility for their own greenhouse gas reductions. Although these measures are extremely valuable, without the coordinated effort of all the developed nations and the major developing ones, keeping global temperatures to tolerable levels is unlikely. Getting all nations on board with emissions reductions is the only way to achieve the greenhouse gas emissions reductions necessary to significantly impact rising temperatures.

Mitigation and Adaptation

Climatologists and other scientists warn that significant reductions in greenhouse gas emissions must begin now if dangerous climate change is to be avoided. The Union of Concerned Scientists Web site states, "With aggressive emission reductions as well as flexibility in adapting to those changes we cannot avoid, we have a small window in which to avoid truly dangerous warming and provide future generations with a sustainable world. This will require immediate and sustained action to reduce our heat-trapping emissions through increased energy efficiency, expanding our use of renewable energy, and slowing deforestation (among other solutions)." This chapter looks at improving energy efficiency, researching and developing different energy technologies, and advancing some technologically unconventional ideas to change the warming trajectory the Earth is now on. The final section describes adaptations that need to be made for those consequences of climate change that are already inevitable.

STEP ONE: IMPROVE ENERGY EFFICIENCY

The easiest and quickest way to reduce greenhouse gas emissions is to radically improve energy efficiency. Encouraging conservation, supporting the use of more energy-efficient technologies, and developing better technologies are some of the ways to reduce emissions of CO_2 and other greenhouse gases.

Encouraging Energy Efficiency

Money is often an effective motivator, and economists agree that a good way to encourage energy conservation is with taxes. A **carbon tax** is a surcharge that is placed on the use of energy sources that release CO_2 into the atmosphere. This tax can, for example, be added to the pump price of gasoline or onto the electrical bill for households and businesses that rely on coal-fired power plants. The more energy consumers use, the more tax they pay. The less energy they use, the less their tax bill. The tax gives people an economic incentive to be more energy efficient by driving less, purchasing fuel-efficient vehicles, buying energy-efficient appliances, and keeping the heat turned down. The money collected can be used for research on alternative fuels and to develop mass transit systems, among other things. Because a carbon tax gives people and companies a financial incentive to conserve energy, industry has an incentive to produce more energy-efficient vehicles and appliances.

Sweden, Finland, Norway, and the Netherlands all collect carbon taxes. Sweden, for example, requires a user-paid surcharge of $150 per ton of carbon released. Some climate scientists are calling for the establishment of a carbon tax in the United States, and the discussion of a carbon tax has begun in political circles. Opponents say that energy taxes are regressive because they force poor people to pay a larger percentage of their income in tax. But the tax could be made revenue-neutral, meaning that it could be used to offset other taxes paid by the public. For example, a fuel tax that replaced some percentage of income taxes would put a surcharge on people's behavior instead of on their hard work. People might be given credits if they live far from where they work. The tax could be increased slowly over time, rewarding those consumers who make lasting changes in their lifestyle by, for example, purchasing energy-efficient vehicles and appliances.

Reducing fossil fuel use has the added benefit of reducing the pollution and the environmental degradation that comes from mining coal and pumping and transporting oil. A reduction in oil consumption would also have important economic and political implications, leading to the reduction of both the trade deficit and the nation's dependence on foreign oil.

In June 2007, the United States Senate approved legislation that requires a 10 mpg (4.25 km/l) increase in the average fuel economy of all vehicles produced over the next ten years. The United States government could go a step further by more rapidly increasing fuel economy standards for its enormous vehicle fleet and requiring increased energy efficiency in government buildings. Requiring better fuel efficiency in such a large market would provide enormous incentive for vehicle manufacturers and many other industries to develop more energy-efficient products. The mass production of more fuel-efficient products would result in improvements in technology and would make the products available at competitive prices for individual consumers.

Developing Strategies and Technologies That Are Here or Within Reach

Energy cannot be created: It merely changes form. Gasoline, for example, is ancient solar energy that was stored in plants. Transforming energy from one form to another is extremely inefficient. A car burning gasoline, for example, gets only about 20% of the energy contained in the gas—the rest is lost as waste heat. Air conditioning systems running on electricity are no better. With this much inefficiency, one fairly easy way to reduce greenhouse gas emissions is to improve technologies to increase energy efficiency.

Transportation is the largest user of energy in the United States. Fuel efficiency is related largely to a vehicle's weight: The heavier the vehicle, the more energy is needed to propel it, and the more energy gets wasted. Encouraging people to drive smaller, lighter cars can help. Research is going into constructing vehicles of the lightweight carbon composite used in race cars that could operate with a smaller, lighter engine and a lighter drive train and assembly. Estimates are that a car built of these materials could weigh 65% less than a modern passenger car, which would greatly improve fuel efficiency.

Hybrid vehicles are already available and are increasing in popularity. Hybrids run the energy lost during braking through an electric motor and into a rechargeable battery. Energy from the battery then boosts the car during acceleration and uphill travel. Because of the additional energy source, hybrids have smaller engines and so are lighter than conventional cars. Some hybrid cars get nearly 50 mpg (21 km per liter). In the near future, hybrid cars will have large batteries that can be plugged into an electrical outlet overnight to increase the charge available for the next day's driving.

Reducing energy consumption also reduces emissions of some non-CO_2 greenhouse gases, and most can be reduced in other ways as well. Chlorofluorocarbons (CFCs) have already been phased out in developed nations and are being phased out in developing countries because of the damage they do to the stratospheric ozone layer: Their contribution to global warming will be negligible by about 2050.

Some known agricultural practices can reduce methane (CH_4) emissions. Rice farmers can use certain plant strains, fertilizers, and only intermittent irrigation. Better feed can reduce CH_4 emissions from cows, goats, and sheep. Techniques to keep methane from escaping landfills, coal and oil mines, and waste management lagoons are being developed. Because methane is an energy source, CH_4 can be captured from landfills or animal wastes and converted to electricity. This technology was pioneered in the United States more than 20 years ago and is now widely used in Europe and elsewhere.

Improving energy efficiency is an important part of reducing greenhouse gas emissions. During the energy crises of the 1970s, when fuel from the Middle East was restricted for political reasons, automakers

The Capitol Steel Mill, the largest polluter and emitter of toxic gases in Beijing, China, dominates the west side of the city. *(© Gary Braasch, from the book* Earth Under Fire: How Global Warming Is Changing the World, *University of California Press, 2007)*

nearly doubled the average efficiency of automobiles, and global growth of CO_2 fell from 4% per year to between 1% and 2%. Because Europe emits half as much CO_2 per unit of GNP as the United States, a large improvement in energy efficiency should be easily attainable. Developing countries such as China and India produce much more CO_2 per unit of GNP than the developed countries; but with technological assistance, they could easily lower their CO_2 emissions per unit of GNP.

Still, according to the report *Avoiding Dangerous Climate Change*, improvements in energy efficiency cannot make up for increases in energy use in the developing nations due to their burgeoning populations and economic growth. In the long run, even greater reductions in emissions will be needed to control greenhouse warming. The next step, then, must be a shift from away from a carbon-based economy.

STEP TWO: TRANSFORM ENERGY TECHNOLOGY

Experts suggest that to substantially reduce greenhouse gas emissions, society must make a massive change in the way energy is produced and used. By the middle of the century, humanity must make a transformation to energy sources that produce zero-carbon emissions. That is, society must move away from an economy based on the use of carbon-based fuels, called the **carbon economy**, to an economy based on **sustainable** energy sources, which are those that can be used without compromising the needs of future generations.

Developing Technologies to Reduce Greenhouse Gas Emissions

Zero-carbon and lower carbon energy sources that are already in use—solar, hydro, wind, geothermal, nuclear, and biofuels—could be improved and in some cases expanded. Solar energy taps the Sun directly rather than indirectly, as with fossil fuels. With the proper technology, solar energy can efficiently heat water or a building. **Photovoltaic cells**, also known as solar cells, convert sunlight directly into electricity. Solar cells arranged in solar panels on rooftops can provide energy to a building. Producing large amounts of electricity requires building huge arrays of solar cells into panels, parabolic troughs, thermal dishes, or power towers. Solar energy is renewable and produces no pollutants or greenhouse gases. The potential for solar power is enormous, particularly in sunny locations such as the southwestern United States.

Hydropower plants harness the energy of water falling over a dam, which spins the blades of a turbine to produce electricity. Hydroelectric energy is renewable and pollutant and greenhouse gas free. While hydropower produces about 24% of the world's electricity, it cannot be further cultivated in developed countries because their rivers are almost all dammed. In developing nations, there are still free-flowing rivers that can be dammed, although people sometimes object to hydropower development because the water that backs up behind dams may flood regions that are of scenic or social value.

Wind energy is renewable, is nonpolluting, produces no greenhouse gases, and is widely available. To create usable power, wind turns turbine blades that are connected to a generator that transfers the energy into usable electrical current. Small wind turbines can be placed individually in open areas, but the large-scale use of wind energy requires a wind farm. Wind farms can be located anywhere conditions are good. Offshore wind farms supply about seven times as much energy in the same amount of area as land-based farms, although the machinery is more prone to corrosion.

Wind energy has enormous potential. Estimates are that wind could supply 40 times the current demand for electricity and about 5 times the global consumption of power. Although wind currently only generates about 1% of global power usage, that amount represents more than a fourfold increase between 2000 and 2006. Technological improvements have brought down the cost of building wind plants by 80%, making wind arrays less expensive to build than any other type of power plant. Wind energy is still more expensive to generate than fossil fuel or nuclear power, but when the entire cost to health and the environment is factored in, wind is extremely competitive. New wind farms are being planned all over the world and are increasingly popular in the United Kingdom.

Geothermal energy harnesses the power contained in hot rock below Earth's surface. Hot water may flow directly from hot springs, or water can be pumped into a region of hot rock and heated. The steam created by the contact of water with hot rock is then used to generate electricity. Geothermal energy is renewable, nonpolluting, and does not emit greenhouse gases. At the world's largest dry steam geothermal field, located at the Geysers in northern California, sewage effluent from nearby cities is injected into the hot rock found there to create steam.

Research is ongoing on a more advanced geothermal technique, Enhanced Geothermal Systems (EGS), in which boreholes are drilled into rock to a depth of about 6 miles (10 km), a depth routinely drilled by the oil industry. The Massachusetts Institute of Technology reported in 2006 that with improved technology, EGS would be able to supply the world's total energy needs for several thousand years. The steam from the deep holes could be cycled into an existing coal, oil, or nuclear power plant.

Nuclear energy was nearly dead after the 1979 partial core meltdown at the Three Mile Island plant in Pennsylvania and the 1986 explosion and meltdown at Chernobyl, Ukraine. Several European countries abandoned the use of nuclear power entirely, and the United States and countries in other parts of Europe halted the construction of new nuclear power plants. But concerns about global warming have brought about a resurgence of interest in nuclear power, which is clean and produces no greenhouse gases.

Nuclear power still has many opponents who question several aspects of its safety: Nuclear power plants have a history of accidents, transporting nuclear materials exposes many people to potentially harmful radiation, and the waste generated is hard to dispose of because it remains radioactive for more than 10,000 years. Proponents of nuclear power say that the technology is well developed, and plants could come online quickly, allowing the world to lessen its reliance on fossil fuels rapidly. Plus, they say, the problems associated with nuclear power plants are being solved: New designs reduce the possibility of catastrophic accidents, and development is under way for the safe disposal of long-lived radioactive wastes for more than the required 10,000 years at Yucca Mountain, Nevada, in the United States. Still, this debate is likely to continue for a long time.

There are two types of nuclear power. **Nuclear fission** power plants use enriched uranium as their energy source. Nuclear power is clean, but the uranium it needs must be mined and is nonrenewable. Current estimates are that if fossil fuels were replaced by nuclear fission, there would be only enough uranium to last anywhere from 6 to 30 years. Uranium can theoretically be collected from seawater, but that technology is a long way off. In a breeder reactor, the byproducts of nuclear fission are made to breed new fuel. No country yet has a functioning breeder reactor, although this research is ongoing.

Nuclear fusion takes place when the nuclei of light elements combine to form heavier elements, just as the Sun fuses hydrogen into helium. Energy produced from nuclear fusion is enormously desirable: clean and very efficient. Fusion reactions produce far more energy per unit of fuel than nuclear fission or any other energy source. For example, 0.04 ounces (1 gram) of nuclear fuel holds the same amount of energy as 2,483 gallons (9,400 liters) of gasoline. Once started, fusion reactions are self-sustaining.

Some of the qualities that make fusion energy attractive also make it problematic. The fusion of two isotopes of hydrogen, deuterium and tritium, takes place at enormously high temperatures of about 180 million °F (100 million °C). In a hydrogen bomb, fusion is initiated by the detonation of a fission bomb, and the reactions proceed until the material runs out. Because a reactor cannot be the site of a nuclear bomb detonation and cannot contain such enormous temperatures, scientists are researching the possibility of a process called cold fusion, which occurs at normal temperatures and pressures. Although progress is being made, there is no guarantee that fusion will be able to replace carbon-producing energy in any significant way by the middle of this century.

Biofuels harness the Sun's energy that is stored in plant and animal tissue. Biomass can be used directly, as when wood, charcoal, or manure is burned to cook food or heat homes. Fuel can also be created by changing the form of biomass. **Ethanol**, for example, is liquid biofuel produced from plant material and can be burned in cars and other vehicles in place of gasoline. Typical ethanol is produced from plant sugar, such as the sugar in corn. Cellulosic ethanol is made from plant fiber, or cellulose, such as corn stalks. Cellulosic ethanol from crop waste could supply about 25% of the energy needed for transportation in the United States while creating about 85% less greenhouse gases than typical gasoline. Biodiesel is another liquid fuel and can be made from fats such as used cooking oil, animal guts, used tires, sewage, and plastic bottles.

Although biofuels burn cleaner than fossil fuels, they are not pollutant free. Ethanol from corn creates about one-third less greenhouse gases than regular gasoline. Because the CO_2 was taken from the environment recently, its addition back into the atmosphere has no net effect (unlike fossil fuels, which emit CO_2 that was sequestered). Because they burn more cleanly than fossil fuels, biofuels are used as a gasoline additive in the United States. One fuel, called E85, is 85% ethanol and 15% gasoline. Ethanol fuel is as much as 25% less efficient than gasoline per gallon.

Biofuels have limits as an alternative fuel source. Cellulosic ethanol is limited by the amount of suitable agricultural waste, which is far less than the amount of fossil fuels used each year. Growing crops to be made into biofuels is extremely inefficient. For example, because fossil fuels are used extensively in pesticides, in fertilizers, and for performing mechanical labor, there is little or no energy gained from biofuels through using crops such as soybeans or rapeseed. Ethanol derived from corn on a large scale is already credited with increasing food prices because corn is a basic crop in much of the food industry, where it is used in a large variety of products, from animal feed to corn syrup.

A 2005 paper by David A. Pimentel of Cornell University and Tad W. Patzek of the University of California, Berkeley, stated that the corn-to-ethanol process powered by fossil fuels consumes 29% more energy than it produces. The results for switchgrass were even worse, the paper said, with a 50% net energy deficit. Dr. Pimentel said in a 2006 interview in *The New York Times*, "Even if we committed 100% of the corn crop to making ethanol, it would only replace 7% of U.S. vehicle fossil fuel use."

Other scientists say that biofuels provide a reasonable alternative to fossil fuels if the right crops are used and ethanol plants become more efficient. Algae contain much more usable oil than land-based crops and could be fed agricultural and other wastes, although at this time research into algae biofuel is in the early stages.

Fuel cells may someday be used in motor vehicles, but will not be ready for mass production for some time. Fuel cells are extremely efficient at harnessing the energy released when hydrogen and oxygen are converted into water. Fuel cells form the basis of what is known as the **hydrogen economy**.

A fuel cell is made of an anode compartment (negative cell) and a cathode compartment (positive cell), which are separated by a porous

The Wrong Direction

Besides concerns about greenhouse gas emissions, fossil fuel supplies are dwindling. Sometime before 2010, society will pass **peak oil.** Peak oil occurs when half of the oil that was ever available for extraction has already been pumped. Although it might seem that a lot of oil would still be left, what remains is generally lower grade, located in remote locations, and harder to extract. Besides that, if the carbon economy continues unaltered, by 2030 the demand for fossil fuels could be nearly 50% higher than it is today, largely due to increased use by developing countries: China's demand is expected to double over 15 years, and India's may double in 30 years. For all of these reasons, the energy industry is looking for other sources of energy, particularly fossil fuels. Two of these possible sources are oil shale and tar sands.

A rock that contains oil that has not migrated into a reservoir is called an **oil shale.** Oil shale is mined in open pits. After mining, the rock is crushed, heated to between 840°F and 930°F (450°C and 500°C), and then washed with enormous amounts of water. This entire process creates petroleum, which can then be extracted from the rock.

The amount of fuel available as oil shale is comparable to the amount remaining in conventional oil reserves.

The United States holds 60% to 70% of the world's oil shale, mostly in the arid regions of Wyoming, Utah, and Colorado. These oil shale resources underlie a total area of 16,000 square miles (40,000 km), a little less than the combined area of Massachusetts and New Hampshire.

Tar sands are rocky materials mixed with oil that is too thick to pump. Tar sands are strip mined, so many tons of overlying rocks are dumped as waste. Separating the oil from the rocky material requires processing with hot water and caustic soda. Tar sands represent as much as 66% of the world's total reserves of oil; about 75% of this reserve is in the Canadian province of Alberta and in Venezuela.

Extraction of both these sources of oil comes with environmental costs. Both require large amounts of water for processing—by chance, many of these deposits are found in arid areas. Plus, since the oil and tar are spread out, the rock must be mined over a large area. Not only does this degrade the landscape and create a large amount of waste rock, environmental restoration after mining is difficult. As for climate change, extracting usable energy from tar sands produces four times as much greenhouse gas as processing the same amount of conventional oil. This is true to a lesser extent of oil shale as well.

disc known as the proton exchange membrane. A catalyst, which aids in chemical reactions, is located on the membrane. The membrane conducts positively charged ions and blocks electrons. In a hydrogen and oxygen fuel cell, pressurized hydrogen gas is sent into the anode compartment, and oxygen gas is sent into the cathode compartment. At the anode, hydrogen gas is forced through the catalyst and is split into electrons and protons. The protons move to the cathode side, and the electrons are conducted through the external circuit to produce electricity. At the cathode, the oxygen gas is sent through the catalyst and splits into two oxygen atoms. These ions have a strong negative charge and attract the two positively charged hydrogen ions and two of the electrons from the external circuit. The catalyst is dipped into each compartment, which assists in the reaction of oxygen and hydrogen. The products of this reaction are water vapor and heat. To convert a significant amount of energy, fuel cells must be stacked together.

Unfortunately, there are many problems with fuel cell technology. Hydrogen does not exist in vast reservoirs, but must be created. It is also difficult to store and use. One solution is to use a reformer, which turns hydrocarbon or alcohol fuels, such as natural gas, propane, or methanol, into hydrogen. Most of the current generation of fuel cells runs on the hydrogen in natural gas. But collecting the compound uses up a great deal of energy and, at this time, produces more CO_2 than burning the fossil fuel directly. Obtaining hydrogen from natural gas decreases fuel cell efficiency and increases the production of waste heat and gases.

Fuel cell technology is promising in other ways. Besides the incredible efficiency when pure hydrogen is used, the oxygen needed for hydrogen-oxygen fuel cells is widely available in the air. However, while vehicles that run with hydrogen fuel cells create no emissions, they do produce CO_2. Unless this gas is sequestered, using hydrogen fuel cells to run vehicles will not solve the global warming problem. Fuel cells that use compounds other than hydrogen are now in development.

While the use of fuel cells is still in its infancy, it is now entering a rapid growth phase, with revenue projected to grow to $15.1 billion by 2014. According to the Society of Automotive Engineers in 2007,

"Fuel cell energy is now expected to replace traditional power sources in coming years—from micro fuel cells to be used in cell phones to high-powered fuel cells for stock car racing." Fuel cells are already replacing batteries in portable electronic devices because they last longer and are rechargeable.

Even so, many drawbacks remain in developing fuel cells as energy sources, as discussed above. Converting hydrogen to another form of energy requires electricity, which must be generated from conventional energy sources with their typical costs. In a 2005 *Science* article, a team of Stanford researchers suggests that these costs would be minimized, and pollutants would be negligible, if the hydrogen was pumped into the fuel cells using wind power. The authors state, "Switching from a fossil-fuel economy to a hydrogen economy would be subject to technological hurdles, the difficulty of creating a new energy infrastructure, and considerable conversion costs but could provide health, environmental, climate, and economic benefits and reduce the reliance on diminishing oil supplies."

Power from coal is so integral to modern society that many energy experts believe that technologies must be developed to make coal burning more environmentally sound. As a result, **clean coal**, which is more efficient and produces far fewer emissions than normal coal, is becoming an important, but controversial, topic. To produce clean coal, emissions from coal-fired power plants are reduced by **gasification**. In gasification, the coal is heated to about 2,500°F (1400°C) under pressure to produce syngas, an energy-rich flammable gas. After cleansing, syngas is combusted in a turbine that drives a generator, and then the waste heat powers a second, steam-powered generator.

Syngas burns cleanly and is easily filtered for pollutants. Overall emissions of most air pollutants from syngas are about 80% less than emissions from traditional coal plants. Greenhouse gas emissions, particularly CO_2, are also lower. Gasification has other positive features: It makes dirty coal usable, which benefits regions where only dirty coal is available. Also, because the gas is cleansed before it is burned, gasification plants don't need expensive scrubbers—the devices that eliminate particulates, SO_2, hydrogen sulfide, and other pollutants from the waste gases. Clean coal can also be liquefied and burned like gasoline.

Gasification has many downsides. A gasification plant costs 15% to 50% more to build and 20% to 30% more to run than a normal coal-fired plant. Due to these additional costs, conversions to clean coal plants will probably not become widespread until industry is given financial incentives or emissions caps. To produce syngas, gasification uses a great deal of energy, about 10% to 40% more than a standard coal-fired power plant. Also, coal mining is very often environmentally damaging. As yet, although gasification has been tested, it has not been used in a full-scale power plant.

Removing Carbon After It Is Emitted

An alternative to reducing greenhouse gas emissions is sequestering the emissions after they have been created. Carbon can be sequestered in natural systems, or technologies can be developed for carbon sequestration.

Natural carbon sequestration can be enhanced, for example, by reforesting on a large scale. Unfortunately, the opposite is happening as enormous expanses of forest are being cleared for slash-and-burn agriculture. Forest preservation and reforestation are economically and politically complex issues.

Another approach to sequestration that has been researched is iron fertilization. In those parts of the ocean where the presence of nutrient iron is limited, scientists have discovered that adding iron dust to the ocean stimulates a plankton bloom. The plankton remove CO_2 from the atmosphere, although for this to work as a means of sequestering carbon, the plankton must then sink out of the system into the deep sea or into seafloor sediments. While small-scale experiments have confirmed that iron fertilization stimulates plankton growth, no one is certain how large-scale fertilization would affect plankton, or how large-scale blooms would affect the oceans. Recent work has shown that there are few locations in the oceans where the plankton would be removed from the system, and climate scientists currently think that iron fertilization will not make much difference to global warming.

Finally, another way to sequester carbon is by increasing the content of organic matter in soils in order to increase the amount of carbon in that soil. Farming techniques that protect soil, such as no-till farming and crop rotation, can help sequester carbon.

Artificial carbon sequestration is another possible approach. CO_2 from power plants and other large sources can be captured and stored. Carbon is easily captured in gasification plants, where CO_2 emissions can be reduced by 80% to 90%, and from natural gas and biofuel plants. Once the CO_2 is captured, it is transported by pipelines or by ship to a storage site. CO_2 can be stored in rock formations, the oceans, or carbonate minerals. The most promising idea is to inject CO_2 into salt layers or coal seams where the gas cannot escape to the surface. (When CO_2 is added to nearly spent oil and gas fields, it actually flushes out some of the uncollected oil.) Reports by the Intergovernmental Panel on Climate Change (IPCC) suggest that sites could be developed that would trap CO_2 for millions of years, with less than a 1% leakage rate for every 1,000 years.

Several sequestration projects are currently under way. Norway is injecting CO_2 from natural gas into a salt formation in the North Sea. CO_2 from a coal gasification plant in North Dakota is being used to enhance oil recovery in a reservoir in Canada. British Petroleum is involved in a project in Algeria that will store 17 million tons of CO_2.

STEP THREE: RESEARCH AND POSSIBLY DEVELOP SOME FAR-OUT IDEAS

Another idea for reducing rising temperatures is to lessen the amount of incoming solar radiation to reduce the amount of energy that enters the Earth system. There are many possible technologies for accomplishing this, and all would require a great deal of research and development to become usable. One crude idea is to enhance global dimming by purposely placing sulfate aerosols in the upper atmosphere. This strategy has a lot of trade-offs, including increased acid rain and negative health effects from pollution, although it would very likely reduce global warming. Incoming solar radiation could also be decreased by increasing cloud cover through cloud seeding.

A more technological solution is to shadow the planet with large orbiting objects. A 1,243-mile-diameter (2,000-km-) glass mirror manufactured from lunar rock, for example, could act as a sort of sunspot. As it orbited Earth, it would reflect back about 2% of incoming solar radiation to compensate approximately for the amount of heating expected from CO_2 doubling. Creating such an object, however, would use a lot of energy.

Tapping into enormous amounts of energy without producing any greenhouse gas emissions is another category of technological solution to global warming. One idea is to place giant photovoltaic arrays on the Moon or in an orbit around Earth. The system would convert solar energy into microwaves and beam the energy to receivers on Earth. A solar plant outside of Earth's atmosphere would receive eight times more solar energy than one inside the atmosphere due to the lack of gases, clouds, or dust to block the sunlight. While these panels would be tremendously expensive, the technology could be extremely effective later this century.

For complex technical solutions to be successful in reducing global warming, at least four things are necessary:

1. The technology must work.
2. The negative consequences (e.g., environmental damage) of the technology must be minimal.
3. The technology must be effective enough to combat the effects of continual increases in greenhouse gas levels.
4. The technology must be less expensive than the cost of reducing emissions at the source.

INDIVIDUAL CONTRIBUTIONS

While avoiding dangerous climate change will require coordinated efforts on a global scale, individuals can make a difference by being conscious of what they do, what they buy, and what actions they take.

People in the developed world lead energy-intensive lives. Energy is used to power up computers, cook meals, drive to soccer practice, and manufacture consumer goods. Reducing energy consumption reduces greenhouse gas emissions. Limiting the consumption of consumer goods, seeking out more energy-efficient technologies, and avoiding activities that use excessive energy are all steps that individuals can take to reduce their impact. Governments can also assist individuals in being more energy efficient by providing monetary incentives for energy conservation.

Energy-Saving Behaviors

Small actions can lead to big energy savings when a large number of people engage in them. A few guidelines for saving energy are:

- Turn electrical appliances off when they are not in use, including lights, televisions, and computers.
- Unplug cell phones and other chargers when not in use.
- Use precise task lighting at night.
- Change old light bulbs to compact fluorescents.
- Keep the thermostat set to a reasonable temperature.
- Always be conscious of ways to reduce energy consumption. For example, take showers instead of baths, and only boil the amount of water needed for cooking.

Because most energy consumption is involved with transportation, and because every gallon of gasoline burned emits 20 pounds (9 kg) of CO_2 (and many other pollutants), conserving energy in transportation is extremely important. If possible, drive less by living near work or school or by using public transportation. Walking, riding a bike, and carpooling are also good ideas. When driving is necessary, avoid energy-wasting behaviors: Keep the car serviced and the tires inflated, drive within the speed limit, accelerate gradually, and avoid drive-through lines.

Energy-Saving Technologies

Choose technologies that are appropriate for the specific task: For example, a small, fuel-efficient car can transport a family to a soccer game as well as a large sport utility vehicle. A clothesline can be used to dry clothes on a sunny day as well as a clothes drier.

Around the house, use energy-efficient appliances and lighting that are operating well. Look for the EPA's Energy Star when choosing energy-efficient products. When possible, switch to more efficient forms of lighting, heating, and cooling. In the long term, encourage and support energy-efficient building design, including renewable energy technologies such as solar panels. Because manufacturing uses a great deal of energy, try purchasing recycled products, which use less energy than products made from new materials.

Vehicle choice is extremely important. Small, energy-efficient vehicles are preferable to larger "gas guzzlers." As gasoline prices rise, alternative vehicles become more popular. Hybrid cars are now widely available, and cars powered by liquid natural gas or fuel cells will be more common in the future.

Some activities waste enormous amounts of energy. For example, burning airplane fuel produces greenhouse gases, while airplane exhaust produces ice crystals that trap them. The total warming effect of air travel is 2.7 times that of the CO_2 emissions alone. Driving or taking a bus or train presents a good alternative.

Be Politically Active

Work with government at all levels to encourage or require energy-efficient behaviors and technologies. Governments can do many things, including:

- Tax energy to encourage conservation and energy efficiency, and to provide funds for research and development of new energy-efficient technologies.
- Develop public transportation and increase the safety of biking by building bike lanes and installing bike racks in public places.
- Provide tax incentives for households and businesses to adopt more energy-efficient strategies or to convert to carbon-free power sources.
- Provide tax incentives for people buying low greenhouse gas–emitting vehicles, while eliminating tax incentives for people buying high-emission vehicles.

⊕ Influence energy-efficient development by designing communities that encourage walking and public transportation use.

Individuals can encourage local politicians to take action on reducing greenhouse gas emissions by promoting energy efficiency, mass transportation, and by developing alternative energy sources. Individuals can vote for national leaders who recognize the potential consequences of climate change and will take action. Political leaders can also be encouraged to see that the United States participates in international treaties that seek to limit greenhouse gas emissions.

Offset Carbon Emissions

People can now pay to offset the carbon they produce. An average car produces about 10,000 pounds (4,535 kg) of CO_2 per year. To offset that amount, a driver can donate $25 to $50 to a carbon-neutral organization. The money helps pay for the development of clean power by subsidizing the construction of new wind turbines or solar energy collectors, for example. Planting trees or buying forestland to preserve it is another way to offset carbon emissions. Organizations can counteract their carbon emissions, too: The Rolling Stones offset carbon emissions from a 2003 concert by donating money for planting trees in Scotland, and Ben & Jerry's ice cream offsets the carbon it produces in manufacturing and retailing. For this strategy to actually offset carbon emissions, the money must fund a project that would not otherwise have been realized.

Buying carbon offsets to counteract greenhouse gas–producing behavior is controversial. Some environmentalists say that buying carbon offsets in conjunction with a conscious effort to reduce an individual's emissions is a way to increase awareness of the global warming problem while supporting projects that may someday help with the solution. But others say that this market approach does nothing to reduce overall greenhouse gas emissions. While it allows people to feel good about contributing money to offset their carbon footprints, most are still engaging in environmentally destructive behaviors. No matter which side of this issue a person takes, there is no doubt that this is a growing business. Estimates are that people are buying more than $100 million per year in offsets, and that the amount is escalating rapidly.

ADAPTATION

Even if a radical reduction in greenhouse gas emissions could be rapidly achieved, temperatures would continue to rise due to greenhouse gases that have already been emitted and the thermal inertia in the climate system. How much temperatures rise depends on what mitigation strategies are developed and when they are begun. In the meantime, people, communities, and nations can respond to environmental changes after they happen, or they can anticipate and prepare for the changes.

Communities and nations differ greatly in the resources they have to protect their people from the impacts of climate change. Poor communities already rarely have enough resources to deal with immediate problems, such as poverty. Poor people lack the access to financial and natural resources and social services and, as a result, are often unable to rebuild their lives after a disaster. For adaptation to climate change to work, wealthier communities will have to assist poorer communities in developing their economies while reducing their greenhouse gas emissions and learning to use alternative technologies.

Adaptation before the predicted changes occur has a large cost benefit. Preparing for a disaster is less expensive and less disruptive to people's lives than mopping up after one. Hurricane Katrina is a tragic example of how planning could have decreased economic costs, the number of lives lost, and the number of those whose lives were disrupted. For decades, climatologists and coastal scientists had warned that a very powerful hurricane could break the levees that protected New Orleans from surrounding water. The levees were designed only to withstand a Category 3 storm. (In the meantime, for a variety of reasons, the city had sunk to 20 feet [6 m] below sea level in some areas.) Despite these warnings, the recommended improvements to the levees were never made. Hurricane Katrina reached Category 5 as it traveled through the Gulf of Mexico but had dwindled to a Category 3 at landfall and was only a Category 1 or 2 as it passed over New Orleans. Although initially people thought that the city had been spared, the storm's slow passage over the region was enough to break the levees. The resulting flood left 1,800 people dead while displacing about one million others from their homes. The economic impact is estimated at as much as $150 billion. By upgrading the levees so that they could have protected against a Category 5 hurricane, New Orleans would have been ready for this inevitable storm and the storm surge that accompanied it. This preparation would have been expensive, but compared to the cost of the damage caused when the levees broke, the cost would have been minor.

Other regions can adapt to climate change by recognizing and preparing for their own potential problems. Healthy ecosystems can protect coastal regions, and the original wetlands that once thrived on the Louisiana coast might have spared New Orleans some of the brunt of the hurricane. Hard structures, such as seawalls, are better used sparingly; but soft protection, such as beach nourishment, is wise, although it is very expensive. Increasing the capacity of rainwater storage systems may reduce the number of times a city floods and can be used to save water for drier times. It is necessary for evacuation plans for residents of storm-prone areas to be well thought out, easy to implement, and understandable by all who need them.

Although this is unlikely to happen until the effects of global warming are even more pronounced, coastal scientists recommend that communities retreat from the shoreline, and that new building takes place farther inland. Insurance companies can help to reduce coastal development by increasing rates for those who live in dangerous areas, as they are beginning to do in the hurricane-vulnerable regions of Florida. Federal insurance, which has allowed coastal development to thrive, can also be eliminated (with some compensation for those who own vulnerable property).

London is the first major world city to recognize the need for a detailed climate change adaptation plan. This old but vital city is mostly built on the floodplain of the River Thames, which is a tidal river. Adaptation to higher water levels began in the early 1970s when a movable barrier was built along the Thames to stop flooding from storm surges. In the early years, the barrier was closed no more than two times per year. In most of the years since 1986, the barriers have been closed between 3 and 19 times. The barrier was designed to mitigate sea level rise until 2030. The city is working on plans for what will come next for flood protection and also on plans for other impacts of climate change, including positive ones. For example, planners anticipate an increase in tourism and recreational activities as weather becomes more favorable in the United Kingdom and less attractive in the Mediterranean region. Some small communities are facing inevitable climate change with similar foresight.

To adapt agricultural systems to a warmer world, agriculturalists may need to develop crop strains that require less water and less soil moisture. Farms may need to be moved to more climatically hospitable areas. Changing the timing of farming events, such as planting crops earlier, will need to continue. In southern Africa, where droughts have become longer, farmers are making changes such as seeking out crops that are better adapted to the current climate, planting trees to protect the soil, and diversifying their livelihoods.

Adaptation will be an effective response to warming only to a certain extent. If no changes in emissions are made, at some point the environmental changes will likely become too overwhelming, and the costs too great. One example is what could happen to South Florida, where a small increase in sea level would flood some of the lowest lying areas and make the coast more vulnerable to damage from hurricanes and other storms. While people may be able to prepare for these changes or at least mop up after large climatic events, this is very draining when it occurs on the scale of a major city, as has been seen in New Orleans. As sea level rises even higher, the entire southern portion of the state of Florida could flood. If this scenario comes true, at some point Floridians will need to give up trying to patch up the damage and relocate. The economic and social costs of doing this for an entire region are unfathomable.

Flood barrier gates on the Thames River are closed when there is a high risk of tidal flooding. Closing the barrier seals off part of the upper Thames with a continuous steel wall. More engineering projects like the Thames barriers will be needed to protect low-lying cities from sea level rise. *(Skyscan / Photo Researchers, Inc.)*

WRAP-UP

Society is a long way from mitigating the problem of climate change. Doing so will require the political will to make the necessary changes to reduce emissions at all levels of human organization, from governments down to individuals. Drastically improving energy efficiency is the easiest change to make and can be rapidly initiated. Technological advances in energy use and even in carbon sequestration should be pursued. Over time, more brazen strategies, such as placing solar panels in space, may be possible. The longer action is delayed, the more drastic future changes will need to be. It is predicted that if society delays action for 20 more years, emissions reductions will need to be 3 to 7 times more than if the reductions begin immediately.

Conclusion

The time of global warming as a controversy is over. Nearly all of the skeptics have come around. Thousands of scientists have gathered and analyzed trillions of bits of data and constructed sophisticated climate models using the world's most powerful computers. They have used those models to explain the environmental changes that are now being observed. And they have arrived at a consensus. The data, the models, the observations, and the anecdotes all point in the same direction: Earth is warming, and human activities are largely to blame.

Scientists mostly agree on this point, too: People must take action on climate change, and they must do it now.

Unfortunately, society has not kept up with the scientists. News reporters still seek out the few remaining skeptics to provide "balance" to their readers, despite the fact that these doubters have largely been discredited. Political leaders see no advantage in recognizing climate change because it is not relevant on the short time frame of an electoral cycle. People are happy to fall back on ideas such as "Well, Earth has been warmer in the past" without knowing what that really means and what the consequences really are. Therefore, while the problem of climate change is moving to the forefront of public consciousness, little organized action has been taken.

Ultimately, climate change cannot be ignored. In human history, people have thrived when the weather was good and suffered and

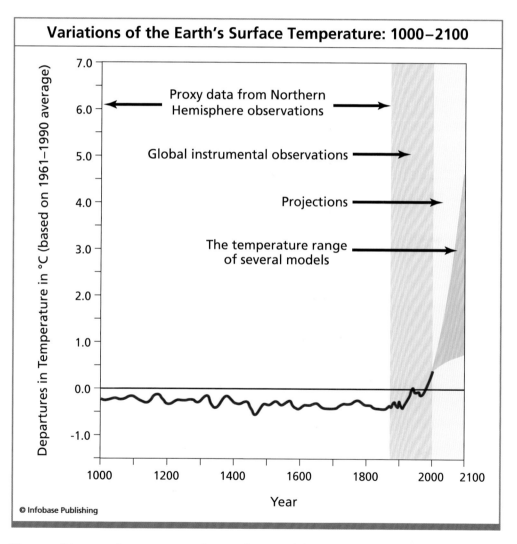

The possible range in temperature from various models projected for the next 100 years is shown relative to the temperature variations of the past 1,000 years.

died when conditions were too dry, too cold, too hot, or too wet. The Vikings prospered on Greenland during the Medieval Warm Period, while at the same time the Maya civilization was collapsing due to a tremendous drought. But the good times did not last for the Vikings once the Little Ice Age arrived and wiped them out of their northern colonies. Cycles of floods and drought have initiated the spread of disease; the demise of past populations due to bubonic plague provides a chilling example.

Today, people may think that they are above the perils posed by global warming, but they are not. Small increases in temperature may benefit some crops in some regions, but that will not be true in other regions. Larger increases in temperature will hurt agriculture almost worldwide. Storms will increase in frequency and intensity, and sea level will rise, causing tens or hundreds of millions of people to become climate refugees. Vulnerable ecosystems—polar, alpine, and coral reef, to name a few—will disappear, as will the many species that will be unable to escape from, or adapt to, the new conditions. It is very unlikely that human society will be able to maintain its population and its lifestyle under these very different circumstances. But these changes are not yet inevitable.

Climate change is a more difficult environmental problem to understand and to fix than most. When a stream of toxic chemicals flows into a river, fish die. A coal-fired power plant visibly pollutes the air, and trees downwind are harmed by acid rain. These problems are visible and their effects immediate. But the buildup of greenhouse gases in the atmosphere cannot be seen and has no immediate consequences. No single event, even one as destructive as Hurricane Katrina, can unequivocally be attributed to it.

Nonetheless, there is a precedent for dealing with a similar environmental problem—a problem caused by substances that do not outwardly appear to be harmful, that bring about consequences that cannot be seen, and that are international in their effect. The problem was ozone depletion, and the cause was the chlorofluorocarbons and other man-made chemicals that caused it. When atmospheric scientists became convinced that these chemicals were causing the

Antarctic ozone hole, the international community responded by phasing out and ultimately eliminating the production of ozone-destroying chemicals. As a result, the rate of increase in the size of the ozone hole is decreasing, and the hole is likely to start healing by the end of this decade.

Solving the climate change problem will take much more effort and sacrifice than solving the relatively simple problem of ozone depletion. After all, the world economy is built on fossil fuel burning, and many portions of the economy benefit from the destruction of the rain forests.

To start dealing with the effects of climate change, climate scientists recommend that society first work toward becoming more energy efficient, and then work toward converting entirely to energy sources that produce zero carbon emissions. They also recommend reductions in the emissions of other greenhouse gases: For example, changing farming practices to reduce methane emissions and stopping the production of man-made chemicals that contribute to greenhouse warming. Finally, they recommend researching and developing more technologically advanced solutions, such as sequestering carbon and harnessing solar energy in space. The important thing is to start making these changes soon, before the temperature rise to which we are committed becomes dangerous.

So far, it has been easy to ignore the environmental effects of climate change, in part because no single incident can be attributed to global warming and because the most serious consequences will not occur until the future. It is easier to deny the contributions people are making to global warming than to recognize and deal with them and make the sacrifices that this will require. The people now in power and those who are now producing most of the greenhouse gas emissions are not the ones who will suffer most of the consequences. The ones who will be most affected by global warming are the young people of today and those yet to be born.

As NASA's James Hansen said in *The New York Review of Books* in July 2006, "Who will pay for the tragic effects of a warming climate? Not the political leaders and business executives I have mentioned.

If we pass the crucial point and tragedies caused by climate change begin to unfold, history will judge harshly the scientists, reporters, special interests, and politicians who failed to protect the planet. But our children will pay the consequences." Because the consequences of global warming will largely be felt by young people, it is especially important for young people to become educated in climate change science and to learn what to do to mitigate climate changes and adapt to them. Young people can voice their dissatisfaction with the political status quo and work to help turn the situation around. It is not too late to begin.

# Glossary

acidification The alteration of seawater so that it becomes more acidic due to increased atmospheric carbon dioxide that ends up in the ocean and creates carbonic acid.

acid rain Rainfall with a pH of less than 5.0. This type of acid precipitation includes acid fog and acid snow.

acids Solutions with free positively charged hydrogen ions that are sour to the taste. Acidic and alkaline solutions neutralize to form salts.

adaptation One of two strategies (the other is mitigation) that can be used by humans to deal with climate change; in adaptation, human behavior adjusts to inevitable changes.

aerosols Solid or liquid pollutants, also called particulates, that are small enough to stay suspended in the air. They can seriously reduce visibility and also cause global dimming, which reduces the amount of solar radiation that reaches the Earth's surface.

air pollution Contamination of the air by particulates and toxic gases in concentrations that can endanger human and environmental health. Some air pollutants are greenhouse gases, and some cause global dimming, which is the reduction of solar radiation that reaches the Earth's surface.

albedo The amount of light that reflects back off a surface; snow and ice have high albedo, mud has low albedo.

algae A very diverse group of mostly aquatic organisms; they are not plants, although some look like plants, and all of them photosynthesize.

alpine glacier   A glacier that grows in the mountains and flows downhill; at its source, snowfall exceeds snowmelt, allowing the glacier to form.

altitude   Vertical distance above or below mean sea level.

aquifer   A rock or soil layer that holds useable groundwater.

Atlantic meridional overturning   Ocean circulation pattern in which dense water in the North Atlantic sinks into the deep sea and pulls warm Gulf Stream waters northward and sends cold saline waters southward.

atmosphere   The gases surrounding a planet or moon.

atom   The smallest unit of a chemical element having the properties of that element.

atomic weight   The sum of an atom's protons and neutrons (electrons have negligible weight).

bacteria   Microscopic single-celled organisms capable of living in an incredible number of environments.

biodiversity   The number of species in a given habitat.

biofuel   Fuel derived from biomass; wood, coal, and manure are natural biofuels; biofuels can also be created from biomass.

biomass   The mass of all the living matter in a given area or volume of a habitat.

carbonate (CO_3)   The composition of the rock limestone used by corals and other animals to make their shells.

carbon cycle   The exchange of carbon between the atmosphere, geosphere (earth), fresh water, oceans, and living things.

carbon dioxide (CO_2)   A molecule made of one carbon and two oxygen atoms that is an important component of the atmosphere and an extremely effective greenhouse gas.

carbon economy   The current economic structure of civilization, which relies on the use of carbon-based fuels, primarily fossil fuels.

carbon sequestration   Storage of carbon in one reservoir so that it is no longer part of the carbon cycle; two natural reservoirs for carbon sequestration are forests and oceans.

carbon tax   A tax placed on energy sources that emit carbon dioxide into the atmosphere; the tax is designed to better pay for the costs of fossil fuel burning and inspire conservation and research and development of non-carbon-based technologies.

chlorofluorocarbon (CFC)   An anthropogenic gas that breaks down the stratospheric ozone and is a potent greenhouse gas; CFC use is being phased out.

clean coal   Coal that has undergone gasification to clean it of pollutants before it is burned.

climate model   A computer simulation of climate constructed by using available data and an understanding of the interactions of the atmosphere, the hydrosphere, and the biosphere; climate models can be used to predict future climate.

climate proxies   Biological or physical artifacts that preserve a record of past temperature; tree ring widths are an example of a biological artifact that reveals the temperature and precipitation conditions that occurred while the tree grew.

climate refugee   A person who is displaced from his home due to climate change; at this time, some Pacific Islanders have been forced to leave their low-lying islands due to rising seas, but many more climate refugees will be created as weather becomes more extreme and seas rise higher.

commitment model   A climate model that predicts what will happen if no additional greenhouse gases are added to the atmosphere and that shows how global and local temperatures will eventually reflect the amount of greenhouse gases already released; these models are not at all realistic, but they provide a base-level idea of what to expect from climate change.

condensation   The change in state of a substance from a gas to a liquid.

continental glacier   A mass of ice, also called an ice cap, that moves outward from a center of accumulation; currently, Earth has two ice caps: Greenland and Antarctica.

convection cells   Currents of air (or water) that rise when warm and sink when cool, forming a closed cell; the major movements of the atmosphere take place in convection cells.

coral bleaching   This results when coral, ordinarily colorful, turns white due to the loss of zooxanthellae; it happens mostly in response to elevated ocean temperatures.

Coriolis effect   The tendency of a moving object to appear to move sideways due to the Earth's rotation.

cryosphere   The portion of the Earth's surface that is frozen water: snow, permafrost, sea ice and icebergs, and glaciers.

dead zone   An ocean region that is hostile to most life, due to a severe depletion in oxygen.

deforestation   The conversion of forest area to nonforest area, often agricultural land or settlements.

desertification   The change of semiarid landscapes into desert, sometimes by a change in natural rainfall patterns but often by the misuse of soil or another human activity.

ecosystem   The interrelationships of the plants and animals of a region and the raw materials that they need to live.

El Niño   A temporary warming of the Pacific Ocean that has implications for global weather patterns; part of the El Niño–Southern Oscillation climate variation.

El Niño–Southern Oscillation (ENSO)   A short-term (in years) climate cycle that oscillates between cold water and low pressure in the eastern Pacific and warm water and high pressure in the western Pacific; the cycle also occurs in the opposite pattern.

electromagnetic waves   The form in which radiation travels; these waves have electrical and magnetic properties.

electron   A negatively charged particle usually found orbiting an atom's nucleus.

element   A substance that cannot be chemically reduced to simpler substances.

environmental refugees   People who have been displaced from their homes by environmental changes; climate refugees are one category of this group.

erosion   The movement of sediments from one location to another by water, wind, ice, or gravity.

ethanol   Liquid biofuel that can be burned in an internal combustion engine; intended as an additive or replacement for gasoline; E85, which is currently on the market, is a mix of 85% ethanol and 15% gasoline.

evaporate   To change from a liquid to a gas, the change of state of a substance from a liquid to a gas, such as the change from liquid water to water vapor, is called evaporation.

evapotranspiration   The loss of water by evaporation from plants.

feedback mechanism   The magnified response of a system to a change; a feedback mechanism can be positive or negative.

firn   Partially compacted snow that has been recrystallized; also called a "névé."

flood basalt   A giant volcanic eruption that coats the land surface with fluid lava that may emit enough gases and particles on a massive scale to bring about a mass extinction.

food web   The set of producer-consumer and predator-prey relationships that make up the biological portion of an ecosystem.

fossil fuels   Ancient plants that have decayed and been transformed into a useable fuel, especially coal and petroleum. These fuels are really stored ancient sunshine.

fuel cell   An energy cell in which chemical energy is converted into electrical energy.

gasification   Integrated gasification combined cycle (IGCC) technology cleans coal before it is burned, increasing efficiency and reducing emissions.

geothermal energy   Energy that comes from hot water; this water is heated in a volcano or in rocks heated in the deep Earth.

glacier A moving mass of ice and snow that forms on land. Glaciers grow when the amount of snow falling in winter exceeds the amount that melts in spring and summer; they shrink when annual snowmelt exceeds snowfall.

global dimming The blocking of incoming sunlight by pollutants so that the planet's atmosphere undergoes cooling.

global warming The worldwide rising of average global temperature; the term usually refers to the temperature increases that have taken place in the past one-and-a-half centuries.

greenhouse effect The trapping of heat that is radiated from the Earth. Without the greenhouse effect, Earth's average temperature would be much lower.

greenhouse gases Gases that absorb heat radiated from the Earth. They include carbon dioxide, methane, ozone, nitrous oxides, and chlorofluorocarbons.

groundwater Water found in soil or rock beneath the ground surface.

gyre Five large ocean currents that travel in a circle around major portions of the ocean basins. They rotate clockwise in the Northern Hemisphere and counterclockwise in the Southern Hemisphere.

habitat The environment in which an organism lives, including climate, resource availability, predators, and many other distinctive features.

heat budget The amount of heat entering and leaving the Earth system; if the amount entering is greater than the amount leaving, the planet warms.

heat capacity The ability of a substance to store heat as it changes temperature; the rate of change of the temperature of a body with the addition of heat.

hurricane Deadly tropical storm characterized by high storm surge, abundant rainfall, and intense winds.

hydrocarbon An organic compound composed of hydrogen and carbon; fossil fuels are hydrocarbons.

hydrogen economy A theoretical system in which hydrogen-based energy, such as that in fuel cells, is used to fuel the economy rather than the fossil fuels used for the carbon economy of today.

hydropower The potential energy of falling water; it can be harnessed by a water wheel, or at a waterfall or hydroelectric dam.

ice cap A mass of ice, also called a continental glacier, that moves outward from a center of accumulation; currently, Earth has two ice caps: Greenland and Antarctica.

ice cores Layers of ice drilled from an ice sheet or glacier that contain an uninterrupted record of temperature, precipitation, the gas composition of the lower atmosphere, and sea surface productivity; these records can go back hundreds of thousands of years.

ice sheet An enormous glacier that covers the land surface and that is greater than 19,305 square miles (50,000 sq. km) in area; the only two ice sheets currently on Earth are the Greenland ice sheet in the Arctic and the much larger Antarctic ice sheet.

ice shelf A floating sheet of ice that projects off a glacier or ice sheet onto coastal waters.

infrared Word used to describe electromagnetic energy with wavelengths longer than red; infrared energy is also known as heat.

insolation Incoming solar radiation that reaches the Earth's atmosphere.

ion An atom that has lost or gained an electron so that it has a positive or negative charge.

isotopes Two or more atoms of the same element having the same number of protons but a different number of neutrons; that is, different atomic mass numbers.

krill Crustacean zooplankton that make up the greatest biomass of any multicellular creature on Earth; an important part of the diet of many marine organisms, particularly in the Antarctic.

La Niña The reverse of an El Niño, in which the surface of the Pacific Ocean off South America is especially cold.

latitude The angular distance of any point on the surface of the Earth north or south of the equator.

Little Ice Age (LIA) The period from about A.D. 1550 to 1850 when temperatures dropped by about 0.9°F (0.5°C) and glaciers advanced. The LIA is loosely correlated with the Maunder Minimum, a period when few to no sunspots appeared on the Sun's surface.

mangrove A flowering tree that grows in dense forests along tropical shorelines and has its roots submerged for part of the day; mangrove ecosystems perform many important environmental services.

mass extinction An event where 25% or more of the planet's species go extinct in a relatively short period of time; this opens many ecological niches for new species to fill and so is a driving force of evolution.

Medieval Warm Period (MWP) A period of time from about A.D. 900 to 1300 in which temperatures were relatively warm and dry; the average global temperature was not nearly as high as average global temperature is today.

methane A hydrocarbon gas (CH_4) that is the major component of natural gas. Methane is also a natural component of the atmosphere and a greenhouse gas.

methane hydrates Water molecules in an unstable icy cage, not held together by chemical bonds, that contain a methane molecule inside; the methane from these hydrates is useable as fuel.

Milankovitch theory The theory that Earth's climate may be determined by the planet's position relative to the Sun; the position varies with respect to the shape of the Earth's orbit (eccentricity), the wobbling of its axis (precession), and the angle of the axis of rotation (tilt).

mitigation One of two strategies (the other is adaptation) that can be used by humans to deal with climate change; mitigation refers to making changes that result in the reduction of greenhouse gas emissions.

molecule The smallest unit of a compound that has all the properties of that compound.

monsoon A seasonally shifting wind pattern between a warm continent and relatively cool ocean in the summer, with a reverse pattern during the winter. Summer monsoons often bring abundant rain.

natural gas   Gaseous hydrocarbons, primarily methane.

negative feedback mechanism   A system response in which a change of variable in the system moves the system in the opposite direction of the variable; e.g., increasing atmospheric CO_2 increases plant growth, which takes up CO_2 and lowers atmospheric CO_2.

neutrons   Uncharged subatomic particles found in an atom's nucleus.

nitrous oxides   NO and N_2O, referred to collectively as NO_x. They are natural components of the atmosphere and are greenhouse gases.

nuclear energy   The energy stored in the nucleus of an atom, which can be released by fission, fusion, or radioactivity.

nuclear fission   This occurs when the nucleus of an atom splits into smaller pieces, accompanied by the release of energy; fission is used in nuclear power plants and nuclear bombs.

nuclear fusion   This occurs when the nuclei of light elements combine to make a heavier element, accompanied by the release of an enormous amount of energy; fusion reactions are self-sustaining but so far are impossible to contain.

nucleus   The center of an atom, composed of protons and neutrons.

oil shale   Sedimentary rock rich in oil that can be mined using heat and enormous quantities of water.

ozone   A molecule composed of three oxygen atoms and symbolized as O_3. Ozone is a pollutant in the lower atmosphere; but in the upper atmosphere, it protects life on the Earth's surface from the Sun's deadly ultraviolet radiation.

ozone hole   A "hole" in the ozone layer where ozone concentrations are diminished; the term usually refers to the Antarctic ozone hole.

ozone layer   The layer, found between 9 and 19 miles (15 and 30 km) up in the stratosphere, where ozone is concentrated; the ozone shields us from the Sun's ultraviolet radiation.

Paleocene-Eocene Thermal Maximum (PETM)   A dramatic and rapid warming of climate that occurred 55 million years ago and is correlated with extremely high atmospheric methane concentrations;

one favored hypothesis is that warmer temperatures melted seabed methane hydrates that entered the atmosphere.

paleoclimatology The study of climate in the prehistoric past; paleoclimatologists use information from ice cores, lake and ocean sediments, and tree rings, among other sources, to reconstruct past climate.

pandemic A disease outbreak, or epidemic, that strikes the entire world or a large portion of it.

particulates Solid or liquid pollutants, also called aerosols, that are small enough to stay suspended in the air. They can seriously reduce visibility and also cause global dimming, which reduces the amount of solar radiation that reaches the Earth's surface.

peak oil The concept that oil production forms a bell-shaped curve with a peak; on the downside of the curve, oil is more difficult to get and more expensive; the term is applicable for an individual oil field, a country's oil reserves, or the entire planet; some scientists speculate that peak oil for the Earth will come (or has come) between 2005 and 2010.

permafrost Permanently frozen soil; common in the polar regions.

pH Numbers from 0 to 14 that express the acidity or alkalinity of a solution. On the pH scale, 7 is neutral, with lower numbers indicating acid and higher numbers indicating base. The most extreme numbers are the most extreme solutions.

phenology The science of the influence of climate on plant and animal life cycles, such as budding or springtime mating.

photons Particles carried by electromagnetic waves that are discrete packets of energy.

photosynthesis The process in which plants use carbon dioxide and water to produce sugar and oxygen. The simplified chemical reaction is $6CO_2 + 12H_2O + \text{solar energy} = C_6H_{12}O_6 + 6O_2 + 6H_2O$.

photovoltaic cells Also known as solar cells, these cells convert sunlight to usable energy.

phytoplankton Microscopic plantlike, usually single-celled, organisms found at the surface of the ocean; they are the planet's single greatest source of oxygen.

plankton Tiny plants (phytoplankton) and animals (zooplankton) that live at the sea surface and form the lower levels of the ocean's food web.

plate tectonics The theory that the Earth's surface is divided into plates that move on the planet's surface; the movements are driven by mantle convection.

Pleistocene Ice Ages (Pleistocene Epoch) The most recent ice age in Earth history (also referred to as the Ice Age) that took place from between 1.8 million and 10,000 years ago; it consists of four glacial and three interglacial periods.

polyp A small cup-shaped animal with a ring of tentacles, such as the coral polyp, that constructs a calcium carbonate structure around itself.

positive feedback mechanism A system response in which a change of variable in the system reinforces that change so that the system moves even more in the same direction; e.g., warmer temperatures melt ice with a high albedo, which gives way to open water with a lower albedo, further increasing temperatures and causing more melting.

precipitation Condensed moisture that falls to the ground as rain, sleet, hail, snow, frost, or dew.

primary productivity The food energy created by producers.

producer An organism that produces food energy from inorganic substances; usually referring to a photosynthesizing plant for food energy.

protons Positively charged subatomic particles found in an atom's nucleus.

radiation The emission and transmission of energy through space or material; also the radiated energy itself.

reflection The return of a light or sound wave from a surface.

respiration The process by which an organism exchanges gases with the environment. Note that in the reaction, sugar and oxygen are converted into CO_2 and water with the release of energy: $C_6H_{12}O_6 + 6O_2 = 6CO_2 + 6H_2O$ + useable energy.

saline Word used to describe water containing salt.

scattering The diffusion or deflection of light as it strikes particles.

sediments Fragments of rocks and minerals that range in size from dust and clay up to boulders.

sedimentary rock One of the three major rock types; sedimentary rocks form from compaction and cementation of sediments or from precipitation of minerals.

slash-and-burn agriculture A practice whereby rain forest plants in the tropics are slashed down and then burned to clear the land for agriculture.

Southern Oscillation The variation in the atmosphere between high and low pressure cells in the eastern and western Pacific, related to the El Niño cycle.

specific heat The amount of energy needed to raise the temperature of 1 gram of material by 1°C.

storm surge Abnormally high sea level due to water being raised up by low atmospheric pressure and by being blown up against land.

stratosphere The upper atmosphere, which rises from top of the troposphere to about 30 miles (45 km) up. The stratosphere contains the ozone layer.

sunspot A magnetic solar storm on the Sun that is seen as a dark spot from Earth; sunspots vary in number on an 11-year cycle; the absence of sunspots during the Maunder Minimum may have caused the Little Ice Age.

sustainable Word used to describe resource use that does not compromise the current needs for resources or those of future generations for present economic gain.

tar sands Sands and rocky materials mixed with oil that can be mined using hot water and caustic soda.

thermal expansion The addition of heat to a liquid causes molecules to vibrate more vigorously, which increases the distances between them and causes the liquid to expand; as the planet warms, thermal expansion will be a significant cause of sea level rise.

thermal inertia The resistance of a substance to a change in temperature; water has higher thermal inertia than rocks.

thermohaline circulation Vertical circulation in the oceans that is driven by density differences between surface and deeper water; seawater density is a function of temperature and salinity.

threshold effect A value beyond which an abrupt response is observed; e.g., if enough Arctic ice melts, so much open water is present that new ice cannot form.

tipping point The point of no return in climate change processes as a result of positive feedbacks.

tree rings Annual layers of a tree's growth that are affected by the temperature and precipitation of each year.

troposphere The lowest layer of the Earth's atmosphere, rising from sea level to about 11 km.

ultraviolet radiation (UV) Short wave, high energy solar radiation; the highest energy wavelengths of UV are extremely harmful to life.

urban heat island effect The phenomenon that urban areas have higher temperatures than nearby rural areas due to the absorption of sunlight and release of heat by ground coverings such as concrete and also to the collection of waste heat.

urbanization An increase in the extent or density of an urban area; the ground surface is covered with man-made substances such as concrete and asphalt that affect the albedo and penetrability of the region.

water cycle The cycling of water between Earth's atmosphere, oceans, and fresh water reservoirs such as glaciers, streams, lakes, and groundwater aquifers.

water vapor Water (H_2O) in its gaseous state.

wavelength The distance from crest to crest or trough to trough in a light or sound wave.

wetland A poorly drained region that is covered all or part of the time with fresh or salt water.

zooplankton   Tiny marine animals that are unable to swim on their own and drift with the currents.

zooxanthellae   Single-celled dinoflagellates (algae) that live in a symbiotic relationship with corals; the zooxanthellae supply oxygen and food to the corals, and the corals supply a home and nutrients (with their wastes) for the algae.

Further Reading

Berzon, Alexandra. "Tuvalu Is Drowning." *Salon*. March 31, 2006. Available online. URL: http://www.salon.com/news/feature/2006/03/31/tuvalu/index.html. Accessed May 28, 2007.

Bowen, Mark. *Thin Ice: Unlocking the Secrets of Climate in the World's Highest Mountains*. New York: Henry Holt, 2005.

Criswell, David R. "Lunar Solar Power System for Energy Prosperity within the 21st Century." World Energy Council (2005). Available online. URL: http://www.worldenergy.org/wec-geis/publications/default/tech_papers/17th_congress/4_1_33.asp#Heading6. Accessed May 28, 2007.

Dean, Cornelia. "Next Victim of Warming: The Beaches." *The New York Times*, June 20, 2006.

Diamond, Jared. *Collapse: How Societies Choose to Fail or Succeed*. New York: Viking Penguin, 2004.

Emanuel, Kerry. *Divine Wind: The History and Science of Hurricanes*. New York: Oxford University Press, 2005.

Environmental Protection Agency (EPA). "Climate Change." Available online. URL: http://epa.gov/climatechange/index.html. Accessed May 28, 2007.

―――― "Energy Star." Available online. URL: http://www.energystar.gov/. Accessed May 28, 2007.

―――― "Green vehicle guide." Available online. URL: http://www.epa.gov/autoemissions/. Accessed May 28, 2007.

Flannery, Tim. *The Weather Makers: How Man Is Changing the Climate and What It Means for Life on Earth*. New York: Atlantic Monthly Press, 2006.

Gore, Al. *An Inconvenient Truth: The Planetary Emergency of Global Warming and What We Can Do About It*. New York: Rodale, 2006.

Hansen, James. "The Threat to the Planet." *The New York Review of Books* 53 (July 13, 2006). Available online. http://www.nybooks.com/articles/19131. Accessed May 28, 2007.

Hansen, James, et al. "Global Warming in the 21st Century: An Alternative Scenario." Goddard Institute for Space Studies, New York, NY (2000). Available online. URL: http://www.giss.nasa.gov/research/features/altscenario/. Accessed May 28, 2007.

Holland, Earle. "First Compilations of Tropical Ice Cores Shows Two Abrupt Global Climate Shifts—One 5,000 Years Ago and One Currently Underway." *Ohio State Research News* (2006). Available online. URL: http://researchnews.osu.edu/archive/lonniepnas.htm. Accessed May 28, 2007.

Linden, Eugene. *The Winds of Change: Climate, Weather, and the Destruction of Civilizations.* New York: Simon and Schuster, 2006.

National Aeronautics and Space Administration (NASA). "Earth Observatory: Atmosphere." Available online. URL: http://earthobservatory.nasa.gov/Topics/atmosphere.html. Accessed May 28, 2007.

Pearce, Fred, and John Gribbin. *Global Warming.* Essential Science Series. New York: Dorling Kindersley Publishing, 2002.

Revkin, Andrew. *The North Pole Was Here: Puzzles and Perils at the Top of the World.* Boston: Kingfisher (Houghton Mifflin), 2006.

Sweeney, Kevin. "Climate of Hope." *Salon.* April 4, 2006. Available online. URL: http://www.salon.com/opinion/feature/2006/04/04/hope/index.html. Accessed May 28, 2007.

Wilkinson, Clive. *Status of Coral Reefs of the World: 2004.* Australian Institute of Marine Science (2004). Available online (downloadable). URL: http://www.aims.gov.au/pages/research/coral-bleaching/scr2004/. Accessed May 28, 2007.

Web Sites

Avoiding Dangerous Climate Change

http://www.stabilisation2005.com

A symposium and report by the Department for Environment, Food and Rural Affairs (DEFRA), United Kingdom.

Carbonfund.org

http://www.carbonfund.org

A nonprofit organization that offers individuals, businesses, and organizations the chance to reduce their climate impact by promoting low-cost carbon reductions and supporting renewable energy, energy efficiency, and reforestation projects.

Chicago Climate Exchange

http://www.chicagoclimatex.com

North America's only, and the world's first, greenhouse gas emission registry, reduction and trading system for all six greenhouse gases.

Educational Global Climate Modeling (*Ed*GCM)

http://edgcm.columbia.edu

Educational information about constructing and using global climate models.

Greenhouse Gas Online

http://www.ghgonline.org

Greenhouse gas science from a greenhouse gas scientist; relates greenhouse gas concentrations to global temperature increases.

Hadley Centre for Climate Prediction and Research

http://www.metoffice.com/research/hadleycentre/index.html

The foremost climate research center in the United Kingdom.

Intergovernmental Panel on Climate Change (IPCC)

http://www.ipcc.ch

Access to reports, speeches, graphics, and other materials from the IPCC.

It's Getting Hot in Here: Dispatches from the Youth Climate Movement

http://www.itsgettinghotinhere.org

Information for young people on the movement to speak out about climate change.

Kyoto Now!

http://www.rso.cornell.edu/kyotonow/index.html

A college student–led group that seeks to make American Universities
commit to reducing greenhouse gas emissions.

Pew Center on Global Climate Change

http://www.pewclimate.org

Climate analysis by business leaders, policy makers, scientists, and
other experts based on sound science; includes the primer Climate
Change 101.

RealClimate

http://www.realclimate.org

Written by working climate scientists for the public and for journalists to
provide content and context for climate change stories.

Index

About the Author

DANA DESONIE, PH.D., has written about the earth, ocean, space, life, and environmental sciences for more than a decade. Her work has appeared in educational lessons, textbooks, and magazines, and on radio and the Web. Her 1996 book, *Cosmic Collisions*, described the importance of asteroids and comets in Earth history and the possible consequences of a future asteroid collision with the planet. Before becoming a science writer, she received a doctorate in oceanography, spending weeks at a time at sea, mostly in the tropics, and one amazing day at the bottom of the Pacific in the research submersible *Alvin*. She now resides in Phoenix, Arizona, with her neuroscientist husband, Miles Orchinik, and their two children.